PRIZE PLAYERS

PRIZE PLAYERS

Michael Coleman

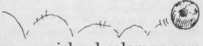

www.michael-coleman.com

Illustrated by
Mike Phillips

Hippo

For Craig Robertson
(especially pages 84–5)

Scholastic Children's Books,
Commonwealth House, 1–19 New Oxford Street,
London WC1A 1NU, UK
A division of Scholastic Ltd
London ~ New York ~ Toronto ~ Sydney ~ Auckland
Mexico City ~ New Delhi ~ Hong Kong

Published in the UK by Scholastic Ltd, 2003

ISBN 0 439 97818 1

Typeset by M Rules
Printed and bound by Nørhaven Paperback A/S, Denmark

2 4 6 8 10 9 7 5 3

INTRODUCTION

Imagine being a professional footballer, running out onto the pitch in front of thousands of cheering fans, scoring loads of spectacular winning goals, holding trophies aloft and winning so many medals you have to buy a big house to put them in. Yes, the life of a football player *can* be fantastic.

But a footballer's life can also be foul. Sometimes players get injured and have to give up playing. Plenty of them go on for years and years with teams who hardly ever win a corner, let alone a trophy. And even the best players will sometimes get booed by the fans and fall out with the team coach...

In this book you'll read about all sorts of players, from the biggest, brightest stars to the not-very-twinkly-at-all kind. Some of them have scooped the game's highest honours, but others haven't done much more than scoop the mud off their boots at the end of the game. Players like...

- The crackpot goalkeeper who threw the ball into his own net.
- The desperate defender who put the boot into his own fans.
- The midfield maestro who played with matchsticks.
- The wild winger who bamboozled opponents with his elastic dribble.
- The stunning striker with the hardest head in the game.

8

But all the players you'll read about have one thing in common. They have made prized contributions to the glorious history of football. In fact some have been so important that they'll be joining the select band who have received one of our coveted *Foul Football* awards. Awards like…

THE "HOW DO I GET OUT OF THIS MESS?" AWARD…

Lomana Lua Lua of Newcastle United who, after being rejected by English league clubs Colchester United and Leyton Orient, found himself working as a loo cleaner at his local McDonald's. Did he let his career go down the pan? No. He pleaded with Colchester to give him another chance and has been flushed with success ever since!

So don't sit there playing about. Award yourself a prize and read on!

LOOT IN THEIR BOOTS

Nowadays top footballers are "professionals". That is, they're paid money – lots of money – to play football. This is why fans think they have a right to boo them and call them rude names. "I'm helping to pay his wages!" they yell, even if they're only watching the match on the telly. It's true, too. A tiny bit of every fan's entrance money or TV licence fee will end up in the players' pockets.

YOU PAID FOR HIM TO MISS THAT PENALTY!

NO I DIDN'T, I PAID FOR HIM TO SCORE A GOAL!

It wasn't always that way, though...

The pro player timeline

1871 The Football Association (FA) Cup competition begins. Until now footballers have played for fun rather than money. There are dire predictions that the competition will change all that, with teams being tempted to pay the best players to join them so they can win the trophy.

1879 Darwen, a tiny Lancashire team, reach the quarter-finals of the FA Cup, losing only in a second replay to the eventual winners, Old Etonians. But suspicions lurk that two of the Darwen players –

Fergus Suter and James Love, both from Scotland – are secret professionals who find money tucked inside their football boots when they get out of their after-match bath.

SORRY, THE BANK RAN OUT OF NOTES.

1884 Preston North End are disqualified from the FA Cup for playing a professional in their team. Burnley support them, saying: "The public will not go to see inferior players. During the first year we did not pay a single player and nobody came to see us."

Defender James Forrest becomes the first professional to play for England. His pay? £1! (Worth just £65 today.) Maybe Dr Edward Morley had something to do with this – Forrest was a Blackburn Rovers player! Also in this year, the first Gentlemen (amateurs) v Players (professionals) match takes place. As if to show how pure they are, the amateurs wear white shirts while the professionals are told to turn up in any colour they like! (The amateurs also win, 1-0).

1885 Faced with a threatened breakaway by Preston, Burnley and 31 other Lancashire clubs, the FA change their mind. Clubs are allowed to have professional players – just so long as they've lived within six miles of the ground for the previous two years.

THE PLAIN SPEAKING BUT DON'T EXPECT TO HAVE MANY FOOTBALLERS FOR FRIENDS AWARD...

Dr Edward Morley, a member of Blackburn Rovers' committee. He didn't agree with the FA decision, saying that in his view full-time footballers were: "money-grabbing, get-rich loafers".

1888 The English Football League is formed. All 12 teams are professional.

1893 The Scottish FA allow professional players. They have to really – to stop any more of them disappearing across the border to England!

1901 A rule is brought in saying that players can't earn more than £4 per week (worth £250 per week today). Known as the "maximum wage", it's still four times as much as a farmhand gets paid.

1909 Footballers form a players' trade union. They're all threatened with being banned from the game but in the end the players win and are allowed to form their union. It doesn't seem to help their cause very much...

1922 The maximum wage, which has slowly risen to

£9 per week (£330 today), is cut to £8 (worth £290)! The players threaten to go on strike – but don't.

1924 Billy Meredith, the famous Welsh winger, retires aged 49. He works out how much he's been paid on average for the 1,100 games he's played for his clubs and country. The answer: £4.75p a week (worth about £110 a week today).

1961 Even though players can now earn a huge £20 per week, they threaten to strike again, and this time really mean it. (Maybe because the real value of their pay has dropped: £20 in 1961 would only be worth £265 today – less than they earned in 1922!) The frightened Football League gives in and abolishes the maximum wage. Fulham and England captain Johnny Haynes becomes the first player to earn £100 per week (worth £1,325 per week today).

Question: Before he won his great pay rise in 1961, Haynes was paid the maximum £20 per week – but not for the whole year. Why not?
a) Players were paid less if they were injured.
b) Players were paid less in the summer.
c) Players were paid less if they missed a match to play for England.

Answer: b) Footballers were only paid their maximum wage during the season. During the summer months they got less – in Haynes's case, only £17 per week (worth £225 per week today).

At this time footballers didn't employ agents to do their talking for them. They were called to the manager's office to sort things out for themselves.

Maurice Cook, one of Johnny Haynes's team-mates, tried an interesting argument during his meeting...

Since the maximum was scrapped, players' wages have risen and risen. In 2001, David Beckham of Manchester United (and, like Haynes, captain of England) earned himself a new pay deal – £80,000 per week!

Where will it all end? Perhaps it already has. In November 2002, the big clubs held a meeting to decide what to do about the huge wages players were now earning. What did they agree? To try to work towards introducing a maximum wage!

THE "MY DAD HOPES I'M GOING TO BE A PRIZE PLAYER AND EARN LOADS OF MONEY ONE DAY" AWARD...

Jean-Pierre Grenier who, in 2002, was invited to special training sessions with Newcastle United at the tender age of... six!

Going, going, gone!

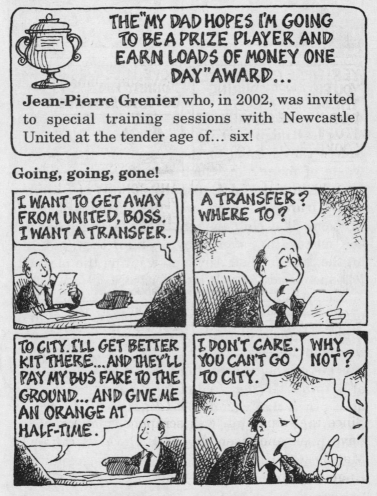

15

Once players started being paid money to kick a football around it was obvious that some of them would want to play for clubs who paid them the most. It was equally obvious that the clubs paying them less might not want their players to leave – unless they'd come to the conclusion they were a waste of money, in which case they'd be only too happy to see the back of them.

The transfer system was designed to solve the problem. If a club thought a player wasn't worth the money they were paying him, they put him on the transfer list. Any club wanting the player to join them had to pay a transfer fee.

The system worked for the players as well – kind of. If Sammy Superbrat wanted to leave his club he could ask for a transfer. If the club agreed, then he was put on the transfer list at a price. If they didn't agree, then that was it. He had to stay – for ever! Until 1960, players were made to sign contracts that gave their clubs the right to hang on to them for life.

Frightening fees

Everybody knows transfer fees have gone up, but how quickly has it happened? Here are some milestone transfers involving English clubs. In which year did the transfers take place – and how much would the fee be worth today?

Transfer fee	Player	Year?	Worth today?
£1,000	Alf Common (Sunderland to Middlesbrough)		
£10,000+	David Jack (Bolton Wanderers to Arsenal)		
£100,000+	Denis Law (Manchester City to Torino, Italy)		
£1,000,000+	Trevor Francis (Birmingham City to Notts Forest)		
£10,000,000+	Alan Shearer (Blackburn Rovers to Newcastle United)		

Answers:
£1,000 – 1905 – worth about £65,000 today. Alf Common was a skilful forward and an England international. People were shocked at the size of the fee. "Where will it all end?" said one newspaper. But England player Billy Bassett of West Bromwich Albion had no doubts: "I should say he was cheap because it was generally thought that he saved Middlesbrough from sinking into the Second League."

£10,000+ – 1928 – worth about £450,000 today. David Jack was an FA Cup phenomenon. In 1923 he'd scored the first ever goal in a Wembley Cup Final. He'd scored again in the 1926 Final as Bolton won 1-0. So was Arsenal's money (actually £10,890) well spent? Definitely. After just one year with Jack in the team, Arsenal were the FA Cup winners!

£100,000+ – 1961 – worth about £1,325,000 today. Did Italian club Torino get a bargain when they bought Manchester City's ace striker Denis Law? They didn't think so. Law was back in Manchester a year later ... but with United! City were able to crow that their rivals had had to pay out more money (£115,000) to get him – but for years it was their one consolation. With Law scoring 171 goals in 309 games, both clubs knew that dynamic Dennis had been worth every penny. Only when Law rejoined City did they have reason to rejoice. In the final game of the

1973–1974 season a goal from Dennis condemned their opponents to relegation. And who were those opponents? Manchester United!

£1,000,000+ – 1979 – worth about £5 million today. Trevor Francis had been a youth star, scoring stacks of goals for Birmingham City. Nottingham Forest's strange manager Brian Clough paid a record British fee – only to stop Francis getting a big head by making him play his debut game in Forest's third team! A year later, though, Francis proved his worth by scoring Forest's winning goal in the European Cup Final.

UK £10,000,000+ – 1996. As England's captain, Alan Shearer actually cost a then world-record **£15 million – worth about £17 million today.** As he's banged in plenty of goals for Newcastle ever since, they've got no doubts he was worth the money. But in an early training session, Newcastle's then manager Kevin Keegan couldn't have been too sure. He'd decided to teach Shearer a trick he'd used when he was a player. An hour later, Keegan had given up – Shearer couldn't do it!

THE MOST APPEALING TRANSFER ADVERTISEMENT AWARD...

Watford FC. In 1983 the Watford squad had been so badly hit by injuries they put an advertisement for new players in *The Times*, "...men or women ... preference given to applicants with two arms and two legs in working order."

Transfer tales

Some transfers are successes, some are failures and a few are just plain different – like this selection from around the world.

● Charlie Buchan moved from Sunderland to Arsenal in 1925 and proved to be not only a penalty-box star but a brainbox star as well. In those days the centre-half used to attack, but Buchan told Arsenal manager Herbert Chapman that he thought theirs should simply defend. Chapman ignored him until Arsenal were belted 7-0 by Newcastle. When he finally took up Buchan's suggestion Arsenal went on a winning streak and ended the season second in the league. Buchan was a prize player who kept on thinking even after he'd retired from football. He started a very successful magazine called *Charles Buchan's Football Monthly*.

● Jan Ceulemans had just been voted Belgian Footballer of the Year in 1981 and was all ready to move to AC Milan until somebody persuaded him to stay. Who, his manager? No, it was his mum! She thought he should stay at home. Ceulemans did, playing his whole career in the Belgian league and being voted Footballer of the Year two more times.

● Luis del Sol was a Real Madrid player until, in 1962, he was transferred to Juventus. Why? Because Real were trying to scrape up enough money to bid for the Brazilian superstar Pelé! The incident left Luis laughing, though. Pelé decided to stay in Brazil.

- Arsenio Erico was transferred by accident! In 1932, aged 17, he was playing in a fund-raising game in Argentina in support of the charity Red Cross, not knowing that the bosses of Argentine club Independiete were watching. They were so impressed that they signed Erico straight after the game. And his fee? Nothing more than a donation to the Red Cross charity!

ALL WE ASK FOR ARSENIO IS THAT YOU FILL OUR HUMBLE COLLECTING TIN.

- Gheorge Hagi is probably the most famous Romanian player ever. He was first picked for his country at the age of 18 and stayed in the team for the next 15 years. He started off playing with a team called Sportul Studentse until his transfer to the top Romanian side Steaua Bucharest. Did Steaua get their money's worth? Definitely: they refused to pay any fee for Hagi at all! What's more, there was nothing Sportul could do about it, because the tough-guy Romanian ruler Nicolae Ceaucescu was a Steaua supporter and director!

- Coen Moulijn, a superstar in Holland, was treated in a quite different way. From the late 1950s he played for Dutch club Feyenoord, staying with them until 1972, by which time he'd helped them become European Cup winners and World Club champions. How come he was never transferred to a bigger club for lots of money? Because the Dutch Federation had made Feyenoord put a line in Moulijn's contract saying they'd never do it!

THE "LET'S BE HONEST, YOU MAY THINK I'M WORTH ALL THAT TRANSFER MONEY BUT I'M BLOWED IF I DO" AWARD...

Jaap Stam, Dutch international, who said after Manchester United bought him from PSV Eindhoven for £10 million in 1998: "Of course it's too much for a footballer. I've seen shopping centres built for less." (Three years later Stam was sold to Lazio in Italy for an even bigger shopping centre: £16 million!)

I'M NOT A SHOPPING CENTRE!

The quids quiz

With past players earning a lot less than the stars of today it's no surprise that many of them tried earning extra money. Some managed it without a problem, but others earned themselves a packet of trouble. Can you sort the good boys from the bad in this collection?

a) Denis Compton, who played for Arsenal (1940s and 1950s) was a real slicker – he made money using his head! **Good boy or bad boy?**

b) James Cowan, who played for Aston Villa's champion team in the 1890s, used his speed off the mark to make money. **Good boy or bad boy?**

c) Vivian Woodward played for Chelsea, Tottenham and England (1900s and 1910s). He couldn't accept money because he was an amateur, but he was allowed to claim his fares back. **Good boy or bad boy?**

d) Luigi Allemandi played full-back for Italian club Juventus. After a 1927 game against Torino, in which Allemandi was reckoned to be man of the match, he was accused of accepting a bribe. **Good boy or bad boy?**

e) Alex James, an Arsenal star in the 1930s, made extra money by trading in boots. **Good boy or bad boy?**

f) Jimmy Warner was Aston Villa's goalkeeper when they were surprisingly beaten 3-0 by West Bromwich Albion in the 1892 FA Cup Final. Not only had Warner played badly, it was later said he'd been taking money from a man. **Good boy or bad boy?**

g) In the 1960s, Sheffield Wednesday and England stars Peter Swan and Tony Kay had a little scheme going which they only told one of their team-mates about, striker David Layne. **Good boys or bad boys?**

Answers:

a) Good boy. Compton advertised the hair lotion Brylcreem. He was the glamour boy of his day. Compton also played cricket for England – so you could say he was never stumped for ideas about how to make money!

b) Bad boy. As well as being a prize player Cowan was a prize sprinter. He was fast enough to take part in professional races and win the prize money on offer. The trouble came when he won a big race after his club had given him time off to rest – because he was supposed to be injured!

c) Good boy. Woodward wouldn't accept a penny, not even his bus fare!

d) Bad boy ... AND good boy. Allemandi was found guilty and banned for a year. A later investigation discovered that he'd been a good boy after all. His ban was scrapped and he went on to win the World Cup with Italy in 1934.

e) Good boy. To top up his wages, James worked one day a week in the boot and shoe department of top London store Selfridge's.

I PICKED THEM UP CHEAP.

f) Bad boy. According to Aston Villa, anyway. Warner admitted he'd had a bet on the game, but said he'd put money on Villa to win. Nobody was able to prove otherwise ... but for some reason Warner never played for Villa again!

g) VERY bad boys. In fact probably the baddest the English game has known. Kay, Swan and Layne belonged to a group who made betting money out of deliberately losing matches. In 1965 they were all sent to prison and banned from football for life.

THE SORRY I CAN'T ACCEPT IT AWARD...

Tony Rougier of Reading was twice caught in September 2000 giving away bottles of champagne. There was nothing suspicious about it, though. Rougier had won them for being "Man of the Match" – only to give them straight back again because he didn't drink!

CRACKPOT 'KEEPERS

They say you have to be mad to be a goalkeeper. They say goalkeepers only play in their position because they're no good at tackling or scoring goals. Get ready to meet some goalkeepers who could certainly tackle, goalkeepers who could score goals – and a few who definitely drove their team's supporters mad!

Careless hands and safe hands

Gary Sprake played in goal for Leeds United and Wales (1960s and 1970s). He had a habit of making some wonderful saves and then spoiling it all by doing something totally crazy.

Do you want to be a better goalkeeper? Then use your mind, hands and eyes at all times – but *not* in the way Sprake did in a big match against Liverpool in 1971...

HE COLLECTED THE BALL SAFELY...

HE THOUGHT ABOUT HOW HE COULD GET LEEDS QUICKLY ONTO THE ATTACK.

HE SAW HIS RIGHT-BACK, PAUL REANEY, IN THE CLEAR...

HE DREW HIS ARM BACK TO THROW THE BALL TO HIM...

THEN SAW A LIVERPOOL FORWARD RACING IN TO COVER, SO CHANGED HIS MIND...

PULLED HIS ARM ROUND AT THE LAST MINUTE...

BUT FORGOT TO HANG ON TO THE BALL...

AND THREW IT IN HIS OWN NET!

Gleefully, the Liverpool fans burst into a song that was doing well in the charts at that time. It was called ... "Careless Hands"!

David Seaman bravely entitled his autobiography *Safe Hands* and, in 1990–1991, they certainly were. That season safe Seaman let in a mere 19 goals as Arsenal went on to become league champions. He'd joined them from Queens Park Rangers for a fee (£1.3 million) which at the time made him the most expensive goalkeeper in England, and since then he's played loads of safe games for both them and England.

He's best known for another two S-words, though: shoot-outs and sniffing. His penalty saves during the 1996 European Championships against Scotland and in the penalty shoot-outs against Spain and Germany turned him into a national hero. But when he let a soft free-kick go over his head against Brazil in the 2002 World Cup he ended the match in tears, even though all his team-mates said the goal was a freak.

But then David Seaman always has been a goalkeeper who showed his emotions. His first game for his junior school team ended in tears as well. His team lost 26-0 and sad Seaman had let in 14 of the goals – in one half!

Banks of England

Gordon Banks was a coal delivery man before turning professional and becoming a red-hot World Cup winner as England's goalkeeper in 1966. So rarely did he make a mistake, forwards began to say he was "as safe as the Banks of England". In other words, instead of driving his team's supporters mad he did it to opposing forwards.

Here's what the famous Brazilian player Pelé said about Banks after he'd made his most famous save, during England's game against Brazil in the 1970 World Cup:

"At that moment I hated him more than any man in soccer..."

although Pelé then added:

"...but when I cooled down I had to applaud him with my heart."

Do you want to be a better goalkeeper? Then see if you can recreate Gordon Banks's famous save in your next playground match:

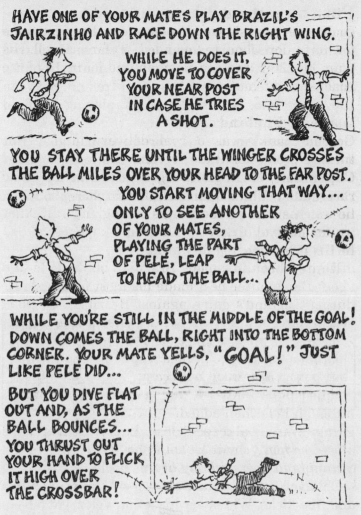

HAVE ONE OF YOUR MATES PLAY BRAZIL'S JAIRZINHO AND RACE DOWN THE RIGHT WING. WHILE HE DOES IT, YOU MOVE TO COVER YOUR NEAR POST IN CASE HE TRIES A SHOT.

YOU STAY THERE UNTIL THE WINGER CROSSES THE BALL MILES OVER YOUR HEAD TO THE FAR POST. YOU START MOVING THAT WAY... ONLY TO SEE ANOTHER OF YOUR MATES, PLAYING THE PART OF PELÉ, LEAP TO HEAD THE BALL...

WHILE YOU'RE STILL IN THE MIDDLE OF THE GOAL! DOWN COMES THE BALL, RIGHT INTO THE BOTTOM CORNER. YOUR MATE YELLS, "GOAL!" JUST LIKE PELÉ DID...

BUT YOU DIVE FLAT OUT AND, AS THE BALL BOUNCES... YOU THRUST OUT YOUR HAND TO FLICK IT HIGH OVER THE CROSSBAR!

That save became known as "The Save of the Century" and, not surprisingly, made Gordon Banks world-famous. He retired in 1972 after losing an eye in a car crash. In all he'd played 73 times for England – and kept clean sheets in nearly half of them (35)!

Pat the cat and hot-shot Jose

Goalkeepers aren't meant to score goals, but quite a few have. Pat Jennings was one of them. He played most of his 1,097 games for Tottenham Hotspur, Arsenal and his country, Northern Ireland, between 1962 and 1986. He won 119 caps, playing his final international at the age of 41.

In all those games Pat scored just one goal. But *what* a goal! It was at Old Trafford, against Manchester United, in the 1967 Charity (now Community) Shield game. But from whereabouts on the pitch did he score it?

a) The halfway line.

b) His goal area.

c) United's penalty spot.

Answer: b) Arsenal had a strong wind behind them – so strong that when Jennings kicked the ball out of his hands it soared almost the length of the pitch, bouncing over a surprised Alex Stepney in the Manchester United goal, and landed in the net!

Paraguayan goalkeeper Jose Luis Chilavert has scored so many goals he could have been put in the *Stunning Strikers* section of this book!

Chilavert's total comes to over 50, from penalties and free-kicks. Whenever his team, Velez, get a free-kick in an Argentinian league match, it's cheerful Chilavert who takes it. If you want to be a better goalkeeper *and* a better goalscorer, then follow Chilavert's example. He practises by taking 120 free-kicks every day!

Chilavert has had plenty fired at him at the other end of the pitch, too – and not only shots. During one league match he had a smoke bomb thrown at him by a rival fan. When the game was replayed on the orders of the Argentinian FA, Chilavert was pelted once again. What was thrown at him this time?

a) Hot-dogs.

b) Cigarettes.

c) Flowers.

Answer: c) It was the fans' way of saying they were sorry for what happened. Cheerful Chilavert picked them up and took them home to his wife!

THE GREAT AT STOPPING SHOTS AND DODGING MISSILES BUT DOESN'T WANT TO KNOW WHEN IT COMES TO CATCHING BUBBLES AWARD...

Peter Schmeichel. Denmark's goalkeeper was also Manchester United's star shot-stopper when they won the treble of Premier League, FA Cup and European Cup in 1998–1999. Out on the pitch he was fearless, but when the team got back to the dressing room and began celebrating it was a different matter. He'd cover his clothes in case they were splashed by champagne!

The 'keepers quiz

Try these questions about famous goalkeepers. Can you grab a good score with both hands or will the right answers whizz right past you?

1 Albert Iremonger played in goal for Notts County (1905–1926). During one match in 1923 he was badly fouled by another player named Ernie Islip. The two players had a punch-up and Islip was sent off. What happened to Iremonger?

a) He carried on playing.

b) He was sent off too.

c) He was carried off unconscious.

2 Fabien Barthez joined Manchester United in 2000. His goalkeeping exploits soon had the Tesco supermarket company asking him to advertise one of their products. What was it?

a) SUPER GLUE   **b)** CARPET SWEEPER   **c)** BUTTER

3 Dino Zoff played for Napoli and Juventus and was Italy's goalkeeper no less than 112 times – an Italian record. Between September 1973 and June 1974 he set a world record, though. What was it?

a) Longest period without letting in a goal.

b) Oldest goalkeeper to score a penalty in an international.

c) First goalkeeper to captain his country.

4 Billy Foulke, one of whose nicknames was "Tiny", was Chelsea's first goalkeeper when the club joined the Football League in 1905. It was due to him that Chelsea stationed little boys behind his goal. Why were they there?

a) To shout encouraging things at Foulke during the game.

b) To stop Foulke tiring himself out retrieving the ball when it went behind.

c) To put opposing forwards off by making Foulke look bigger.

5 John Burridge played for Aston Villa (and 17 other clubs!) from the 1970s onwards. What special technique did he have for keeping himself alert?

a) Leaping up to touch high branches on trees.

b) Having oranges thrown at him when he wasn't expecting it.

c) Helping a farmer round up runaway piglets.

6 Thomas Ravelli, goalkeeper for IFK Gothenburg and his country, Sweden, has got a good reason for having a big head. What is it?

a) He holds the record for stitches in his head.

b) He holds the record for international caps.

c) He holds the record for goalkeepers scoring headers from a corner.

7 Elisha Scott was Liverpool's goalkeeper from 1912–1934, helping them become champions in 1922 and 1923 and playing 429 league games in all. What did he spend an hour doing before each of those games?

a) Soaking his goalkeeping gloves in water until they felt right.

b) Sitting on the loo reading the match programme.

c) Throwing a ball against the dressing room wall and catching it.

8 Bert Trautmann joined Manchester City in 1946. But when City signed him there were protest marches in Manchester with fans threatening not to turn up to watch the team play. What didn't they like about poor Bert?

a) His nationality.

b) His mohican hairstyle.

c) The team he used to play for.

9 Back in the 1890s and 1900s, Jack Robinson was goalkeeper for Derby County and England. He was very strict about his diet, insisting that before a game he should eat – what?

A PLATE OF LOW-CALORIE SPAGHETTI

A JAR OF PICKLED ONIONS

A BOWL OF RICE PUDDING

10 During one war-time England match Charlton's Sam Bartram had to be told to leave the pitch by a policeman. Why?

a) There was an air-raid expected.

b) The game had ended and he hadn't realized.

c) He'd been arrested.

Answers:

1 a) Islip was a twit. He'd picked on one of the tallest goalkeepers ever. Iremonger stood 6 feet 6 inches (almost 2 metres) in his football socks and was well able to look after himself. Not only did Islip get sent off, an irate Iremonger gave him two broken ribs as well.

2 c) Barthez had made a few bad mistakes. He turned the offer down. The fans were calling him "Butterfingers Barthez" already!

3 a) Zoff didn't let in a goal for over 12 matches, a total of 1,143 minutes. A bit better than his debut match in goal for his first club Udinese – that day Zoff let in five!

4 c) Foulke's nickname of "Tiny" was a joke. His other nickname was "Fatty", because by the time he joined Chelsea he weighed in at a massive 22 stone (nearly 140 kg) and had reached 23 stone (nearly 160 kg) by the end of his goalkeeping career in 1907. As if that sight wasn't terrifying enough, Chelsea thought putting small boys behind his goal would make Foulke look even bigger! Answer **b)** is definitely wrong. The fact that Chelsea had also invented ball-boys to fetch the ball back when it went off was an accident.

5 b) The thrower was his wife. She had been trained to fire oranges at Burridge when he was least expecting them.

NOT WHEN I'M ASLEEP, DEAR!

6 b) In 1995 Ravelli beat the existing record of 125 held by England's Peter Shilton and went on to earn 143 caps before retiring in 1997.

7 c) It was one of Scott's two ways of warming up. The other way was to wear woolly gloves, two pairs of socks and three woolly sweaters. That was in good weather! When winter came along and the pitches were hard he added a pair of long johns under his shorts and bulky knee pads!

8 a) City signed him straight after World War II had ended – and Trautmann was a German. He'd been captured in Germany and brought to England. The team he'd been playing for when City spotted him was the Camp 50 Eleven, the football team of the prisoner-of-war camp where he'd been imprisoned. It all worked out well in the end. Brave Bert was City's goalkeeper for 15 years, helping them win the FA Cup in 1956, even though he ended the match with a broken neck!

9 c) Robinson had a favourite saying: "No pudding, no points". His team-mates believed him, too. When Robinson didn't get his usual helping before their match against Sunderland on the opening day of the 1894–1895 season, Derby were whacked 8-0!

10 b) It had gradually been getting foggier and foggier, with Sam able to see less and less of what was happening. It was only when a policeman tapped him on the shoulder and told him everybody else had gone off that Bartram discovered the match had been abandoned without him knowing!

THE NOT VERY GOOD AT GIVING INSTRUCTIONS AWARD...

Frank Swift, Manchester City's goalkeeper who, aged 19, famously fainted at the end of the 1934 FA Cup Final when he realized his team had won. During the Second World War, when professional football was abandoned, Swift served as a special police constable. But the first time he was sent out to direct traffic he got so confused he ended up walking away and leaving the traffic to sort itself out!

Prize pen-pix: amazing Arthur Wharton

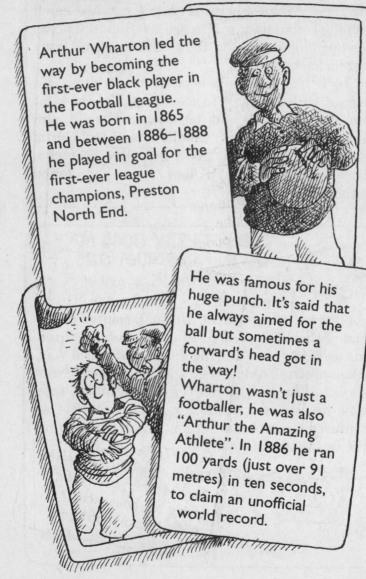

Arthur Wharton led the way by becoming the first-ever black player in the Football League. He was born in 1865 and between 1886–1888 he played in goal for the first-ever league champions, Preston North End.

He was famous for his huge punch. It's said that he always aimed for the ball but sometimes a forward's head got in the way!

Wharton wasn't just a footballer, he was also "Arthur the Amazing Athlete". In 1886 he ran 100 yards (just over 91 metres) in ten seconds, to claim an unofficial world record.

Two years later he turned professional sprinter, winning the unofficial professional championship, the Sheffield Handicap.

As a sprinter, Arthur's temper could be as quick as his feet. He was once placed second in a race he thought he'd won. When awarded his consolation prize, a salad bowl, he smashed it on the ground!

As a footballer, Arthur Wharton was a bit of an acrobat and definitely a show-off. A fan wrote to a newspaper describing one trick: "I saw Wharton jump, take hold of the crossbar and catch the ball between his legs!" In 1997 the BBC filmed Shaka Hislop, then Newcastle's goalkeeper, trying to repeat this trick. It took him ages!

THE AUTOBIOGRAPHY QUIZ

Nowadays the top players don't just win medals and international caps – they have books published about their lives as well. Most footballers don't write their own books, they have a "ghost writer" to do it for them. The writer will interview the player, find out all the facts about them and then set about tackling the really difficult part: coming up with a title!

Could you do it? Have you got what it takes to turn out top titles? Find out in this quiz. Use the words in this list to complete the titles of each prize player's life story:

Ball, Bubbly, Gray, Hard, Run, Second,
Skin, Top, Walk

a) Craig Johnston (Liverpool, 1980s) was an all-action midfield man who scored important goals for his team. He also had hair which covered his ears – so it's surprising that he was able to hear two of the words of the Liverpool anthem and use them as his title.

b) Tommy Smith (Liverpool, 1970s) never did this sort of terrible tackle to any of his opponents, ho-ho.

40

c) Ron Harris (Chelsea, 1960s and 1970s) gloried in the nickname "Chopper" – and not because he flew to games by helicopter.

d) Mick Channon (Southampton, Manchester City and England, 1970s) was another flyer. He now trains racehorses to do the same.

e) John Barnes (Watford, Liverpool and England, 1980s and 1990s) was a tricky winger who was always on the receiving end of a lot of nasty chanting about the fact that he was black.

f) Andy Gray (Dundee United, Aston Villa, Wolves, Everton and Scotland, 1970s and 1980s) was a crunching striker. Nowadays he's always on TV as a match analyser and general know-all. His book title would have been even better if it had been written in the days of black-and-white television!

g) Alan Ball (Everton, Blackpool, Arsenal, Southampton and England, 1960s, 1970s and 1980s). England's all-action World Cup-winning midfield man wins the prize for the book with the most obvious title!

h) George Best (Manchester United and Northern Ireland, 1960s and 1970s) was a wild-living winger whose picture was always in the newspapers – either with a ball at his feet or with a glass of champagne in his hand.

i) Billy Bremner (Leeds United and Scotland, 1960s and 1970s) was a fiery midfield man who loved to win – which was a pity, because Leeds were runners-up a lot more often than they were winners.

Answers:

a) *Walk Alone* ... and in one way Johnston was right. In 1986 he led the way by becoming the first Australian footballer to appear in an FA Cup Final.

b) *Over the Top – Anfield Secrets*

c) *Soccer the Hard Way*

d) *Man on the Run* ... especially during one match being covered by the television company ITV and their top commentator Brian Moore. Channon had bet on a horse that was running in a race taking place during the match, so he asked Moore to give him a thumbs-up sign if it won. When Moore did just that, Channon proceeded to gallop round the pitch smacking himself on the behind!

e) *Out of his Skin*. Barnes was amazing, never letting the terrible actions of some football crowds get to him. When, on one occasion, a banana was thrown at him he simply picked it up and ate it.

f) *Shades of Gray*. (Even though TV was all in colour by then!)

g) *It's All About a Ball*

h) *The Good, the Bad and the Bubbly*

i) *You Get Nowt for Being Second*

DESPERATE DEFENDERS

Some defenders look pretty desperate all of the time. But as a defender's number one job is to stop the other team's forwards scoring, even the coolest defender will get desperate some of the time – as you'll discover with this selection of prize players who've performed right back in defence (and left back, and in the centre, and defensive midfield as well!).

Winning Franco and fearless Wilf

"Franco" Baresi spent his whole career with Italian club AC Milan, making his debut in 1978 and going on to win six Serie A championships, three European Cups and two World Club Cups. (No wonder he didn't want to leave!) He was so popular that when he retired something else retired with him. What was it?

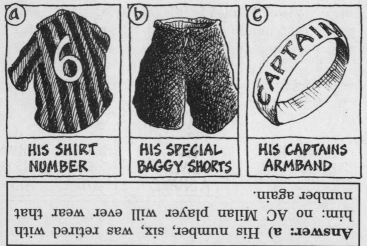

ⓐ	ⓑ	ⓒ
HIS SHIRT NUMBER	HIS SPECIAL BAGGY SHORTS	HIS CAPTAINS ARMBAND

Answer: a) His number, six, was retired with him: no AC Milan player will ever wear that number again.

Baresi played many times for Italy. His greatest day was captaining his country in the World Cup Final of 1994 – even though few had expected him to be fit in time. Bullet-hard Baresi had had an operation on his knee just two weeks before the finals began!

Wilf Copping was a member of Arsenal's triumphant team of the 1930s. Famed for his crushing tackles, Copping was known as "Fearless Wilf". He loved to see forwards quivering with fear at the very thought of copping one from him so on match days Wilf tried to look extra-tough. How?

Answer: b) He obviously hoped the forwards would worry about him roughing them up!

Andoni the 'acker and villainous Vinnie

Andoni Goikoetxea played for Spanish side Atletico Bilbao. In 1983 his team were up against Barcelona, who had Argentine superstar Diego Maradona on their side. This is how Maradona described a Goikoetxea tackle in that game: "I put on a turn of speed against him, beat him, toed it, and when I went to trap the ball, turn and take off again, crack, the axe from behind. I felt like my leg was trapped, like it was completely wrecked."

Maradona's ankle had been broken. Goikoetxea was banned for 16 games and from then on was known as – what?

a) The Spanish Slaughterer.

b) Maradona's Mangler.

c) The Butcher of Bilbao.

Answer: c) Did Goikoetxea regret his tackle? Hardly. He lovingly installed the boots he was wearing that day in a glass cabinet at home!

Vinnie Jones was a desperate defender with Wimbledon. He hit the headlines when he was caught on camera squeezing Newcastle's Paul

Gascoigne's dangly bits during a match. Afterwards, to show there were no hard feelings, Gascoigne sent Jones a present. What was it?

a) A "kiss me quick" hat.

b) A flower.

c) A Valentine's card.

Answer: b) Perhaps he was suggesting that Jones was really a bit of a pansy! The defender did his best to prove otherwise. Wimbledon had signed him from non-league Wealdstone. There he once more performed like a desperado defender. After drinking too much he was locked up in a police cell all night, being let out just in time to go straight to Wealdstone's match – without his football boots. Jones had to borrow a pair, but they were a size too big. The first time he kicked the ball during the warm-up one of them came off and flew into the crowd! Arnie Reed, the physiotherapist at Wealdstone had Jones sized up all right:

"He's incredibly loyal. Ask him to jump off the stand roof and he'd do it. But he's as thick as two short planks. He always grabbed the quiz book on our coach trips so that he could ask the questions. That way he didn't have to answer."

47

Masterful McCracken and record Rio

Bill McCracken was unusual. Many desperate defenders try to bend the laws of the game – but McCracken actually managed to change them! He played for Newcastle and Northern Ireland from the 1900s until he retired in 1923. By then the fans of every other team were delighted to see him go because it meant their ears wouldn't be pulverised by the sound of the referee's whistle every time Newcastle were defending. Why? What was McCracken an expert at?

a) Catching forwards offside.

b) Pretending a forward had fouled him.

c) Sneakily grabbing a forward's shirt.

Answer: a) The rule then was that when a forward got the ball he had to have three players between him and the other team's goal. McCracken was an expert at scuttling out of defence at just the right time to scuttle an attack and win an offside decision. McCracken never lost this ability to spot a good forward. He was still acting as a talent scout when he was 90!

Rio Ferdinand is a record-breaker and that's for sure. When it comes to transfer fees it's usually stunning strikers who break the bank, but in August 2002 Manchester United broke the world record for a defender by signing England's Rio Ferdinand from Leeds United for £30 million! Why? This is what one of his previous managers said about him:

> *"I believe he will develop into the best central defender in world football."*

– West Ham manager, Harry Redknapp

Unfortunately Rio's career with his new team began badly. He strained a knee and had to miss the opening part of the 2002–2003 season. How did he do it?

a) Putting his feet up.
b) Putting his best foot forward.
c) Putting his foot in it.

Answer: a) Rio was resting! He was watching television and had his foot up on the coffee table. There must have been a good film on or something because restful Rio was sitting like that for some time. When he stopped putting his feet up he found he couldn't put them down again without it hurting.

49

Balletic Bobby, dandy Daniel and terrible Tommy

Bobby Moore, captain of England's 1966 World Cup-winning team, was one of the few defenders you couldn't call desperate. His old rival, Brazil's Pelé, called Moore "the finest defender in the world" because he always seemed unhurried and rarely lost out in a tackle. Tottenham Hotspur striker Jimmy Greaves once gave Moore a jolt in a league match though. As his team won a corner, Greaves raced into the penalty area and – did what to Moore?

a) Jumped on his back.

b) Started dancing with him.

c) Pulled his shorts down.

Answer: b) Greaves linked his arm in Moore's and made the England captain do a graceful twirl on the penalty spot.

JIMMY'S PLANNING TO LEAD SOMEBODY A MERRY DANCE TODAY!

Daniel Passarella was a defender who made other defenders feel desperate because he wouldn't stop scoring goals himself. In 298 matches in the Argentine league, Dead-eye Dan scored no fewer than 99 goals and banged in another 22 goals in his

70 international matches for Argentina. He didn't stop scoring when he moved to Italy to play for Fiorentina and Inter Milan; Dan's the man who still holds the Italian League record for goals scored by a defender. When he became Argentina's manager, though, Passarella decided he wanted something from his players other than goals. What was it?

a) Manicured fingernails.

b) Short hairstyle.

c) Shaved legs.

Answer: b) Yes, Passarella insisted on his players having a bit off the top, which they thought was a "bit off" – because they'd all seen photographs of Passarella in his playing days, with hair down to his shoulders!

Tommy Smith played for Liverpool in the 1970s. He was a tough defender who never liked missing a game if he could help it. After getting injured one week, Smith appeared with his leg strapped up and said to his manager, Bill Shankly, "I'm prepared to take the chance. It's my leg." What did Shankly say in reply?

a) "It's not your leg, son."

b) "Yes, son – it's a broken leg!"

c) "What you going to do, son – hop?"

Answer: a) So whose leg was it? "It's Liverpool Football Club's leg!" said Shankly. Iron-man Smith was soon back in the side, though – which may explain why on Merseyside both he and Shankly were regarded as leg-ends!

51

Prize pen-pix: fearsome Frank Barson

Frank Barson played for, amongst others, Aston Villa and Manchester United in the 1910s and 1920s. Was he hard? You bet. Villa team-mate Billy Walker said of him, "Frank helped me – but he had no friends on the field." Barson was an honest player, though. If he was out to get somebody, he often told the ref he was going to do it!

One referee who stood up to him was a man named Jack Howcraft, who was in charge of the 1920 FA Cup Final between Villa and Huddersfield Town. "One bad foul and you're off," he told Barson. Frank played cleanly and picked up a winner's medal.

One day he missed his train and had to walk seven miles to get to the ground in time. Even so, all the newspapers said he played a great game. When United played Aston Villa, Frank came up against old team-mate Billy Walker ... tackled him ... and put him in hospital for three weeks!

Before one game a good luck message arrived from two more of Frank's friends, brothers named Fowler. Were they footballers? No, they were murderers in prison, waiting to be hanged. Barson had a determined streak all right. It was rumoured that after being offered a rotten rise by his manager he turned up for their next meeting with a gun in his pocket!

As an incentive to get him to sign for them, Manchester United promised to buy Barson a pub if the team achieved promotion within three years. They did, but on the first night friendly Frank decided running a pub wasn't for him – so he gave it away! Frank stayed fearsome to the end. In the final game of his career he was sent off.

THE INJURED FEELINGS QUIZ

Getting injured is all part of the game for any prize player. Ask Darren Anderton of Tottenham Hotspur and England. He used to be out of action so often the other players nicknamed him "Sick-note"! But in 1997–1998 it seemed that quite a few players weren't simply getting injured naturally but had been cursed – by the BBC! Their football highlights programme *Match of the Day* had filmed a new opening sequence. Here are some of the stars it featured – and what the curse did to them...

- Top striker Alan Shearer was crocked before the season even began and the first highlights programme was shown!
- The same went for Southampton's Matthew Le Tissier. He broke his arm and couldn't even use the TV handset to tune in.
- With the action only just under way, Roy Keane of Manchester United injured his knee (trying to injure somebody else's) and didn't play again that season.
- Robbie Fowler of Liverpool missed the start of the season and then, when he did come back, was injured again.
- With his team storming up the league, Arsenal striker Ian Wright was congratulating himself on dodging the curse when he was crocked and had to miss the final crucial games which took Arsenal to the league championship.
- And it even went wrong for a manager. The sequence showed the then Wimbledon manager

Joe Kinnear thumping a table as he "encouraged" his team. Before the season had ended Kinnear was in hospital after suffering a heart attack.

Here are eight further facts about soccer sufferers and immobilising injuries. Can you sort out the True from the False?

1 Alan Wright of Aston Villa suffered a knee injury in 1996. It was caused by riding a bicycle. **True or false?**

2 Giancarlo Antognoni was playing for Fiorentina against Genoa when he was thumped on the side of the head by Genoa's goalkeeper. Antognoni collapsed and his heart stopped beating for half a minute. **True or false?**
3 On holiday in Majorca in 1981, Davie Provan of Celtic fell asleep on a hard sunbed. When he woke up he had an injured knee. **True or false?**
4 As a player, Jack Wheeler of Notts County didn't miss a single game in 26 years. **True or false?**
5 Frantisek Planicka was Czechoslovakia's goalkeeper in the 1934 and 1938 World Cups.

In 1938, he played 15 minutes of a quarter-final match against Brazil with a broken arm. **True or false?**
6 Arsenal and England goalkeeper David Seaman once injured himself changing channels on his TV. **True or False?**

7 Jimmy McPhail played for Celtic in the 1950s. In 1998, then aged 70, McPhail took the club to court, blaming them for the fact that he'd started to lose his memory. **True or false?**
8 After hurting his foot in 1999, Moroccan international Mustapha Hadji revealed how he treated an injury – he stuffed a lump of raw onion down his sock. **True or False?**

Answers:
1 False. Prize players don't ride bicycles! Wright's knee injury was caused by the cramp and discomfort of driving his fabulous Ferrari car.
2 True. Antognoni had suffered a double fracture of the skull and internal bleeding. He came back to play for Fiorentina, though, which may explain why he was such a crowd favourite. Injuries dogged him throughout his career. After helping Italy win their 1982 World Cup semi-final, he had to miss the final with a cut ankle. Ag-ony for Antognoni!

3 True. His knee had swollen up and needed two operations to fix it.

4 False. Wheeler didn't miss a single game in 26 years as Notts County's *trainer*. Mind you, he always was a healthy man. He was Huddersfield's goalkeeper in 1952–1953 when they won promotion to the top division and he didn't miss a game all season.

5 False. Planicka's achievement was three times as amazing – at a time when substitutes weren't allowed he played all 45 minutes of the second half with a broken arm!

6 True. He strained his back!

7 True. McPhail claimed that he'd headed the ball so much during his career it had damaged his brain. (Even though he lost the case, McPhail might have had a point. He was great in the air. When Celtic beat Rangers 7-1 in the 1957 Scottish League Cup Final, McPhail scored a hat trick of headers. What's more, in 2002 a coroner looking into the death of ex-West Bromwich Albion striker Jeff Astle decided that Astle's brain definitely *had* been damaged by heading the heavy leather footballs they played with at that time.)

8 False. Hadji put a lump of raw steak down his sock. He firmly believed that it beefed up his powers of recovery!

HMMM...

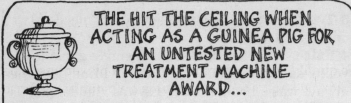

THE HIT THE CEILING WHEN ACTING AS A GUINEA PIG FOR AN UNTESTED NEW TREATMENT MACHINE AWARD...

Jimmy Melia, Liverpool (1960s). When manager Bill Shankly wanted to test a new machine the club had bought for treating injuries, Melia agreed to be the guinea pig. He didn't know the machine worked by giving the player little electric shocks – especially when, as the machine's dial was slowly turned up from 0 to the top setting of ten, Melia didn't feel a thing. Suddenly Shankly realized what was wrong: the machine wasn't plugged in. So, with Melia still attached and the dial still on its top setting, he turned it on...

MIDFIELD MAESTROS

To qualify as a maestro in midfield, a player has to be able to do just about everything: help out his defence by tackling oncoming forwards and also help out his attack by following up and occasionally banging in some goals. On top of that he's got to find enough energy to spray passes to all corners of the pitch.

YOU SAID YOU WANTED TO SEE ME COVER EVERY INCH OF THE GROUND!

Sounds tough? Here are some prize players who have managed it.

The Full Monti
Luis Monti is the only player to have taken part in two World Cup Finals for different countries. He played for Argentina against Uruguay in 1930 (and lost), then for Italy against Czechoslovakia in 1934 (and won). How did he manage this? Because the rules were different then. You could play for the country you were born in or the country you played

in. Monti was born in Buenos Aires and so qualified by birth for Argentina. But, after helping his club Boca Juniors win three Argentine league championships he moved to Juventus (winning four Italian league titles with them!) and so qualified to play for Italy.

What was so special about Lively Luis? You can tell by his nickname. It was "Doble Ancho" which means "twice as wide" – because he covered much more of the pitch than any other player!

Genial Joe

Joe Mercer had a smile as wide as a barn door – and legs that were the complete opposite. They were as skinny as a chicken's and shaped like a couple of bananas. As his Everton team-mate Dixie Dean said: "His legs looked like they wouldn't last a postman his morning round."

Before joining Everton in 1932 he'd played as a teenager for a team called Ellesmere Port. How much was Joe paid for his first game with them?
a) Two pence.
b) A bag of vegetables.
c) Four sausages.

Answer: a) *and* **b)** You could get into the cinema for two pence in those days (even though it would only be worth £1.30 today) and as for the vegetables – Joe really thought he'd hit the bag-time!

Joe stayed with Everton for 15 years, proving to his mum that he'd made the right choice. (When the

60

club had first tried to sign him she'd advised her son to play a few games with Everton's reserves before he made his mind up!) During those years he won a league championship medal and captained England. Then, out of form, carrying a dodgy knee and thinking of giving the game up for good, Mercer was transferred to Arsenal – and his matchstick legs got a new lease of life.

In the eight years Joe was their captain they won the league twice and the FA Cup once. As the Arsenal winger Denis Compton said: "You might be just about ready to drop, but you never did – not with Joe behind you."

Those legs just kept on going, even though for a few seasons in a row Joe had said it was time he retired. Nobody believed him, especially Mrs Mercer who laughed:

"He'll probably go on like this until he's 100 – and then take up blow football!"

Then in April 1954, with Joe not far short of his 40th birthday, he sailed into a tackle in a match against Blackpool at Highbury. The crack was heard by everybody in the ground. Mercer's left leg had been broken. As they stretchered him past the stand, Genial Joe smiled at the crowd and waved goodbye. Those famous legs had played their final game.

Deadly Didi

Brazilian star Didi (his real name was Valdir Pereira) was a World Cup-winning midfield man in both 1958 and 1962. His great talent was in passing the ball. His team-mates used to say: "He can make the ball talk!"

It was said that Didi's passing was so accurate he could land the ball on a coin from any distance (not that it was often called for during matches).

NO, NO! I TOLD YOU TO PRACTICE LANDING A BALL ON A COIN!

"Didi" means "cobra", a snake with a quick and deadly bite. It was a good name, because Didi's opponents often felt as if the same thing had happened to them. Not because he went round biting people, but because Didi had invented an amazingly deadly kind of free-kick. This is what he made the ball do:

- zoom up in the air and over the wall of defenders...
- then, just as it looked like it was sailing over the crossbar too, it would start to dip ...
- ... and bend away from the struggling goalkeeper ...
- ... to drop gently into the goal.

Didi called it his "Fôlha Sêca" (falling leaf) free-kick, but it soon became known as a "banana shot".

So whenever you see a player trying the same thing nowadays you know who invented it – Deadly Didi.

Dynamic Duncan

Sometimes footballers say nasty things about each other. Sometimes they say nice things but don't mean them. Duncan Edwards was a unique case. Nobody ever said anything nasty about him, and when they said nice things they really meant them. Nice things like:

"He'll make a world-beater."

– Joe Mercer, who saw Duncan when he became his coach with the England Schoolboys team.

63

"He is the most complete footballer I have ever seen."

– Sir Matt Busby, the Manchester United manager who signed Edwards.

"If I'd had to choose one footballer to play to save my life, that player would have been Duncan Edwards."

– Sir Bobby Charlton, who played with him.

Duncan Edwards was a phenomenon. He could play equally brilliantly in defence, midfield or attack. He played his first league game for United at the age of 16, before he'd even turned professional. He played his first game for England when he was 18 and won another 17 caps. He won his first League Championship medal with United in 1956, aged 19, and played in an FA Cup Final a year later.

Nowadays you hear players moaning about being tired because of how many games they play. Dynamic Duncan didn't. In the 1956–1957 season he played for Manchester United in the League, FA Cup and European Cup, for England in the British Home International Championship and World Cup qualifying matches, for a Football League team, and went on a three-match tour with the England Under-23 team. How many games did he play in total?

a) 50–60

b) 60–70

c) 70–80

Added to those, like other young men aged 18–20 at that time, he had to serve some time with the Army. Which meant more football! He played games for his Army unit – and they'd never seen anybody who could shoot like him! In the Army Cup semi-final that year, with his team 4-2 down, Duncan moved up to the attack – and hit five goals in 15 minutes!

Everybody who saw him play agreed that he could have become one of the most marvellous midfield maestros in the history of the game. Tragically, it wasn't to be. On 6th February 1958, the plane carrying the Manchester United team back from a European Cup game crashed on take-off at Munich airport. Duncan Edwards fought in hospital like he always had on the pitch, but he died two weeks later. He was just 21 years old.

If you ever go to Dudley in Worcestershire where Duncan Edwards was born, you'll see that his home town is determined to keep his name alive. You'll find an Edwards Road, you'll find a bronze statue in the town centre and if you head for the Parish Church of St Francis you'll find him commemorated in a stained-glass window.

Laughing Len

How often have you watched a game and seen a midfield man do any of these:

- stop in the middle of a mazy run and sit on the ball
- pause and smooth his hair before having a shot
- dribble past the goalkeeper, stop the ball on the line ... then call for another teammate to tap it in
- pass the ball ... but put so much spin on it that it bounces back to him.

Almost certainly never – unless you're old enough to have seen Len Shackleton play. Laughing Len did all these wonderful tricks and more in his career with Bradford Park Avenue, Newcastle and Sunderland in the 1940s and 1950s. No wonder his nickname was *The Clown Prince of Soccer*.

Although he had the most fantastic ball control, Shackleton wasn't very tall, just 5 feet 7 inches (1.7 metres). Neither was he big and beefy. But boy, was he stubborn. Less than a year after he'd left school and signed for Arsenal, their manager, George Allison, told him: "Go back to Yorkshire and get a job, son. You'll never make the grade as a professional footballer."

Stubborn Shackleton only took half Allison's advice. He eventually went back to Yorkshire, in

1940, not to give up football, though, but to sign for his home team, Bradford Park Avenue. Six years later he was picked for England!

Shackleton was one of the most skilful players of his time, and a great goalscorer as well. When he joined Newcastle he scored six goals in his first match as his team thumped Newport 13-0. Ever honest, he said afterwards, "Newport were lucky to get nil!"

Len laughed on the pitch but he could be outspoken off it. He didn't think it right that he could play in front of massive crowds and only be paid £15 a week – and he said so, loudly. This didn't make him popular with the people who ran the game, many of whom also helped pick the England team. It was always thought that this was one of the main reasons he was only picked five times for England.

THE "GET-YOUR-OWN-BACK" AWARD...

Len Shackleton. After retiring Len wrote his autobiography, entitled *Clown Prince of Soccer*. It gave Shackleton the chance to say just what he thought of the people running football clubs – which he did in one of the most famous chapters ever to appear in a football book. It's headed: *Chapter 9 – The Average Director's Knowledge of Football.* And the page below is completely blank!

Prize pen-pix: awesome Alfredo di Stefano

Alfredo Stefano di Stefano Lauhle is born on 4th July 1926 in Argentina. Just as well. If he'd been born in England he'd have been called plain old Fred Stephens, which doesn't sound half as good.
Aged 20, he's part of the forward line for Argentine champions River Plate. It's so good at taking defences apart that they're nicknamed "La Maquina" – The Machine.

In 1949 Alfredo becomes a pirate! Football has stopped in Argentina because the players have gone on strike so he leaves River Plate and heads off to play in a pirate league (that is, not accepted by FIFA, the world football authority) in Colombia for a team called Millonarios.

1953 – and Alfredo's in the dock. He's been sold by Millonarios to Spanish club Real Madrid. Trouble is, he's also been sold by his legal club River Plate to Madrid's deadly rivals Barcelona. A court decides that he should play alternate seasons for each team! He plays a few games for Barcelona. They're not impressed and tell Real Madrid, "You can have him".

Alfredo's first game for Real is a 5-0 win and he scores a hat trick. Their opponents? Barcelona!

It's the start of great times for Real Madrid. They win the European Cup five years in a row, from 1956–1960, with awesome Alfredo scoring in each of the finals.

Di Stefano was a midfield man who liked to be everywhere. He'd help his defence and get forward to score goals.

As Miguel Munoz, his team-mate and – later – coach at Real Madrid, said, "With him in your side you had two players in every position."

Some players are prize-winners from the very beginning. Others give the impression as youngsters that they'll never be good enough to win any prizes at all. They get told "sorry, son" by one team only to find fame and glory with another.

Are you a good judge of talent? Decide which of these players were told "Sign here!" and which were rejected.

1 Ronaldo. World Player of the Year in 1996, World Cup winner with Brazil in 2002 and the tournament's top scorer. **Sign here or Sorry, son?**
2 Diego Maradona, hero of Argentina when he captained his country to World Cup victory in 1978. **Sign here or Sorry, son?**
3 Alan Ball, pint-sized midfield man with Everton, Arsenal and Southampton and, aged 21 as a Blackpool player, the youngest member of England's 1966 World Cup-winning team. **Sign here or Sorry, son?**

HE'S NOT GONNA SCORE MANY HEADERS

4 Billy Wright, top defender for Wolverhampton Wanderers and England's captain, who became the first ever player to win 100 caps for his country. He finished with 105, having missed only three international matches in 13 years. **Sign here or Sorry, son?**

5 Emilio Butragueno played for Real Madrid and Spain throughout the 1980s, twice winning the Prix Bravo as Europe's best young player. He so regularly swooped to score goals that would kill off the other team that he was nicknamed "The Vulture"! **Sign here or Sorry, son?**

6 Johann Cruyff had championship-winning careers with both Ajax, in his home country Holland, and Barcelona. He captained his country to the World Cup Final in 1974 and was the first man to win the European Footballer of the Year three times. **Sign here or Sorry, son?**

7 Mario Kempes won the World Cup's Golden Boot award for being top scorer in the 1978 tournament, hitting six goals as his country (Argentina) went on to win the trophy. **Sign here or Sorry, son?**

8 Norman Whiteside played for Manchester United and Northern Ireland in the 1980s. He made his debut for Northern Ireland after making only two league appearances for United – and in one of those he came on as a substitute! **Sign here or Sorry, son?**

9 Zico (real name Artur Antunes Coimbra) scored 54 goals for his country, Brazil, between 1975–1986, many of them from wicked free-kicks. He played most of his club games with Flamengo, the first when he was 16 and the last when he was 40! In 1981 he helped Flamengo beat Liverpool to win the World Club Championship. **Sign here or Sorry, son?**

IT'S FLAMENGO, NOT FLAMINGO!

Answers:
1 Sorry, son. Ronaldo failed a trial with Brazilian club Flamengo, the first team he tried.
2 Sign here. There was never any doubt that Maradona was going to be a big star. At the age of nine he was ball-juggling on his own TV programme, playing league football at 15 and made his debut for Argentina at the ripe old age of 16!
3 Sorry, son. Ball was sized more like a tennis ball than a football and was told that he was too short to be a footballer. He only managed to make it to 5 feet 6 inches (1.7 metres) when he was fully "grown".
4 Sorry, son. As a 15-year-old on the ground staff, Wright was sent home by Wolves' manager Frank Buckley who told him that he was too short to be a defender. He was then told that Wright was a hard worker and good grass-cutter, so he

invited him back ... and eventually said "Sign here!"

5 Sorry, son. The coaches at Real Madrid didn't think Butragueno was good enough, so they sent him off to play for their lower-class "nursery team" Castilla. They thought Emilio was brillio so they sent him back again – and this time the Real coaches changed their minds.

6 Sign here. Cruyff was taken on by Ajax straight after he'd had a trial as a ten-year-old. They needn't have bothered testing him really. All they needed to do was ask Mrs Cruyff, Johann's mum. She was a cleaner at the Ajax ground and had been the one who'd asked for him to be given the trial in the first place.

7 Sorry, son. Kempes, a gangly teenager with a reputation as a goalscorer, went to top Argentine side Boca Juniors for a trial. They turned him down, so he went to another club – Instituto Cordoba – and they said "Sign here!"

8 Sign here. Whiteside's first Northern Ireland appearance was in the 1982 World Cup – at the age of 17 years and 42 days! That made him the youngest ever player in a World Cup finals match. Unfortunately it was a case of early start, early finish. Injuries forced Whiteside, a cruncher who got crunched in return, to give up the game before he was 30.

9 Sorry, son (almost). The coaches at Flamengo thought Zico didn't weigh enough to be a footballer. So they put him on fattening diets to build him up and made him lift weights until he was stronger ... and then they said "Sign here!"

WILD WINGERS

Anybody who plays out on the wing deserves a prize. There are so many disadvantages. You haven't got so much room to escape from ferocious full-backs for a start, so your ball control has to be really good. You're also closest to the spectators, so sometimes your hearing needs to be really bad!

CAN'T YOU TAKE A BIT OF HONEST CRITICISM?

Dazzling dribblers: Billy Meredith and Sir Stanley Matthews

One winger the fans used to love was Welsh star Billy Meredith. They knew he was great to watch – and sometimes to talk to. Meredith was a star dribbler, and had been since he won a dribbling competition at the age of ten. But when he wasn't whizzing down the wing with the ball at his feet, Meredith didn't believe in running back to help his defence. Instead he'd chat to the crowd until the ball came his way again!

If you were a defender, though, it didn't pay to get too close to him. Nowadays players have to put sticking plaster over wedding rings and anything else that might be dangerous, but in the days when

Meredith played (1894–1924) referees weren't so fussy. That's why he was allowed to play every game with a toothpick clamped between his teeth!

He must have got through a good few toothpicks. Here's what busy Billy got up to in a single week in 1895:

Sat 16 March: boat trip to Belfast to win his first cap for Wales v Northern Ireland.

Mon 18 March: Back to London to play for Wales v England.

Wed 20 March: Up to Manchester to play for his club, Manchester City.

Sat 23 March: On the train to Wrexham for Wales v Scotland.

Question: What did busy Billy do on Tuesday, Thursday and Friday?

The exercise must have kept him pretty fit, though. Meredith continued to be a wild winger until he was 49 years old.

Sir Stanley Matthews was another player who dribbled on ... and on ... and on. Starting in 1932 he played for Blackpool, Stoke City and England until he was even older than Billy Meredith. When he finally hung up his boots he was 50 years old!

I'D HAVE KEPT GOING BUT MY BOOTS HAD HAD ENOUGH.

No wonder one of Matthews' nicknames was "The Ageless Wonder". Another was "The Wizard of Dribble" because it was so difficult to get the ball off of him. How difficult? Here's what other players said about him:

"Playing against Stanley Matthews is like playing against a ghost."

— Johnny Carey, Manchester United and Ireland captain.

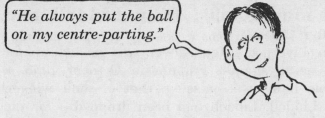

"He always put the ball on my centre-parting."

– Tommy Lawton, an England striker with shiny hair parted in the middle who loved Matthews' accurate passes.

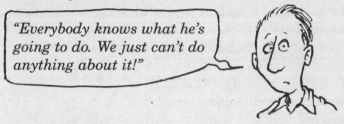

"Everybody knows what he's going to do. We just can't do anything about it!"

– Danny Blanchflower, Tottenham and Northern Ireland captain.

Stanley Matthews' secret was his speed off the mark. In the 1950s there was a joke going round that he could move so fast, he was able to flick the switch on his bedroom wall … and be under the covers before the bulb had gone out!

One-man teams: Billy Liddell and Tom Finney

When Liverpool's team-sheet was posted up for their game against Fulham in October 1958, a notable name was missing: that of their winger, Billy Liddell. Liddell had been dropped – for the first time in 20 years! In all that time he'd only missed a match either because he was injured or because he was playing for his country, Scotland.

Liddell was a quick, powerful winger who liked nothing better than coming up against a full-back who wanted to kick him up in the air. He'd say:

"I enjoy playing against hard tacklers. I play hard myself."

– An interesting remark from a footballer whose first junior team in Scotland were called Lochgelly Violets!

Compared to their successes in the 1970s and 1980s, Liverpool didn't win that much in Liddell's time. With brilliant Billy in the side, they were league champions in 1946–1947 and losing FA Cup finalists in 1949–1950. But, after being relegated in 1954, Liverpool were unable to escape from the old Second Division until 1962. Most modern players would soon be asking for a transfer if their team suffered the same fate, but not Liddell. He stayed with Liverpool. You can tell how much the team depended on him from the nickname they were given at that time. What was it?

a) Liddellpool

b) The Liddell Marvels

c) Billy's Boys

Not bad considering that football wasn't Billy Liddell's main job! He spent much of the week working in an office, as an accountant. He reckoned accountancy made him a better player because it kept his brain active! He'd only have time to train twice a week (instead of every day like the other players) but nobody could have guessed from the way he played.

And when the game was over and Billy Liddell had a bit of free time he didn't sit down and put his feet up but got on with something else. What?

a) Helping run a boys' club.

b) Writing newspaper articles.

c) Lecturing.

d) Teaching at a Sunday school.

e) Serving as a magistrate.

79

Billy Liddell put some of his natural fitness down to the fact that he didn't smoke or drink. When Liverpool won the league in 1947 he even refused to touch a drop of champagne. So imagine his surprise when, after he broke the record for league appearances by a Liverpool player in 1957, the club presented him with … a drinks cabinet!

Liverpool thought the world of Billy Liddell, though. Said the club's then chairman, Tom Williams: "There will never be another like him. He is a model of what every player should be."

Tom Finney (now Sir Tom) was another footballer who did more than kick a ball around. Finney was known as "The Preston Plumber" because as well as spending his whole career player with Preston North End, he also built up a very successful plumbing business.

Finney scored 30 goals in 76 games for England, and 187 goals in 431 league games for Preston. He used to get annoyed when the newspapers said that Preston were a one-man team, but when Finney was injured and had to miss nearly half the 1948–1949 season, what happened? Preston were relegated! His team-mates knew how good he was though. One of them, Ken Horton, said:

> *"We used to get the ball out to Tom as quickly as possible and then run into the box and wait for it to come across. It invariably did, at the right height and the right speed, and we simply had to side-foot it over the line. It was as easy as that, for we were playing with a superman."*

Tom Finney had plenty of chances to leave Preston. In 1948 he'd had a brilliant game for England, scoring twice in a 4-0 thumping of the current World Champions Italy in Turin. Remembering this performance four years later, Italian club Palermo offered Preston £30,000 for Finney – close to the world record for a transfer at that time (even though it would "only" amount to £460,000 today). In addition Finney himself would get a huge fee, big wages, a Mediterranean villa and a luxury car. What did he do? He turned it all down, stayed loyal to Preston and won – what?

a) One League Championship medal.
b) One 2nd Division Championship medal.
c) One FA Cup Winner's medal.

Answer: b) – in 1950–1951 when Preston were promoted again. His only other medal was an FA Cup loser's medal, after his team were beaten 3-2 by West Bromwich Albion in the 1954 final.

So was Finney that good? According to one of his greatest fans, fellow Preston player and later Liverpool manager, Bill Shankly:

"Tom Finney would have been great in any team, in any match and in any age – even if he had been wearing an overcoat!
"He'd have the opposition so frightened they'd have four men marking him when we were kicking in!"

Even the newspapers loved Finney. One said: "If all the brains in the game sat in committee to design the perfect player they would come up with a reincarnation of Tom Finney."

During his long career Finney also proved he wasn't only a wonderful winger, but a star striker as well. After starting out as an inside-left, he'd moved to the right wing for a while, then into the striker's position. Was he any good there? Good enough to play in that position for England! Jimmy McIlroy, the Burnley and Northern Ireland international, said:

"As a right-winger converted from a left-winger, he was the best centre-forward I've ever seen!"

Tom Finney was never booked and never sent off. He was never even spoken to by a referee. He was once photographed touching an official – but even that wasn't anything nasty. It happened before Tom's last game for Preston in 1960. As a way of saying goodbye, the two teams and the officials got together to sing "Old Lang Syne" and Finney found himself holding a linesman's hand!

THE FLYING WINGER AWARD...

Vivian Gibbons, Bristol Rovers. Gibbons was an amateur player for Bristol Rovers who worked as a teacher in London during the week. In September 1932, Gibbons asked to be excused to play in a mid-week evening match. But headmasters were strict in those days and he was refused permission – so the club arranged for an aeroplane to bring Gibbons to the match straight after his last lesson of the day.

Troublesome twisters: Jinky the Flea and the Little King

In September 2002, Celtic fans voted for the club's Greatest Ever Player. The award went to Jimmy Johnstone. During his career, desperate defenders called him lots of things. But his team-mates and the Celtic fans had two nicknames for Johnstone – "the flea", because he was so short, and "Jinky" because of his jinking runs as Celtic's star right winger during the 1960s and 1970s.

C'MON, I'M READY FOR YOU!

In 1967, Celtic became the first British club to win the European Cup. Three years later they reached the final again, after beating the English league champions Leeds United in the semi-final. In that match, Johnstone was up against Leeds and England full-back Terry Cooper. With Jinky at his jinking best Cooper's team-mate, desperate defender Norman Hunter, shouted across some advice on how to deal with him. What was it?

a) "Bite his legs!"

b) "Leave him to me!"

c) "Kick him!"

Strangely for a flying winger, the one thing Jimmy Johnstone *really* hated was ... flying! But with Celtic leading the way for Britain in European competitions in the 1960s it was something he usually couldn't avoid. He managed it once, though. Celtic were playing Hungarian side Red Star Belgrade in the first leg of a tie in 1969. At half-time, with the score 0-0, his manager Jock Stein jokingly told Johnstone that if they managed to win the match by four clear goals he could stay at home for the second leg and not have to fly to Belgrade. What happened? In a sizzling second-half performance Johnstone scored two goals and made three more to help Celtic win 5-1! Afterwards the Flea bounced straight over to his manager and reminded him what he'd said. Happy Stein had to keep his promise.

Roberto Rivelino played in Brazil's winning World Cup side in 1970. Instantly recognizable with his bandit's moustache, he was a winger with a wicked shot. What's more, he could thump them in from any distance. See if you can match this Rivelino record next time you're playing in a school game:

IT'S YOUR KICK-OFF. THE INSTANT THE REFEREE'S WHISTLE BLOWS, MAKE SURE THE BALL IS PASSED TO YOU.

– PEEP!

DON'T DRIBBLE FORWARD, JUST HAVE A SHOT FROM WHERE YOU ARE – YES, JUST ON THE HALF-WAY LINE!

BOOT!

STAND BACK AND WATCH THE BALL SAIL INTO THE BACK OF THE NET.

ASK THE REF HOW LONG IT TOOK. YOU NEED TO HAVE SCORED IN LESS THAN 3 SECONDS TO BEAT RAVELINO'S RECORD!

Yes, that what he did. As his team kicked off, Rivelino spotted that the opposition's goalkeeper was still kneeling down saying his pre-match prayers – so Roberto the Rocket simply whacked the ball in from where he was.

AND PLEASE LET ME KEEP A CLEAN SH...

Thumping free-kicks and long-range shots weren't Roberto's only tricks. His dribbling was pretty good too. This was his special trick. Try it in the back garden – but not near the greenhouse.

DRIBBLE THE BALL FORWARD.

START RUNNING YOUR LEFT FOOT SIDEWAYS OVER THE TOP OF THE BALL, MAKING IT LOOK AS THOUGH YOU'RE SWERVING IT TO THE LEFT (KEEP RUNNING FORWARD THOUGH!)

KEEP MOVING YOUR FOOT UNTIL IT'S PASSED RIGHT OVER THE BALL.

NOW DRAG IT BACK TO THE RIGHT...

LEAVING YOUR DEFENDER LOOKING DESPERATE!

It was called an "elastic dribble" because if you get it right it looks like the ball is on a piece of elastic.

I COULDN'T DO THE TRICKS SO I GREW THE MOUSTACHE INSTEAD.

Rivelino spent most of his career with Brazilian club Corinthians. Like Tom Finney he didn't win a championship medal but the fans loved him to bits. You can tell that from his nickname: Little King of the Park.

The wild quiz

Here's a list of wild facts about ten wingers – but they've all been jumbled up. The words in italics actually go with another fact. Can you sort them out – or will it drive you wild?

1 Manchester United winger George Best was given a four week ban in 1969–1970 because at the end of a match he *put the ball in the net with a back-heel*.

2 Leonel Sanchez played left-wing for Chile in the 1962 World Cup. He's best known for his performance in Chile's match against Italy. After being fouled, Sanchez leapt up and settled the argument by *heading*.

RATS!

4 WEEK BAN

3 Manuel Francisco dos Santos was better known as Garrincha, meaning "Little Bird". This wild and wonderful winger starred for Brazil in their 1958 and 1962 World Cup wins. Yet it was something of a miracle that Garrincha could play at all because after a childhood illness he could *wash his own football kit.*

4 Wingers want to score great goals and West Germany's Pierre Littbarski (1980s) was no exception. He'd lie awake at night dreaming that he'd beaten all ten outfield players, dribbled round the goalkeeper and *knocked the ball out of the referee's hands.*

5 Andrei Kanchelskis scorched down the wing for Manchester United and Everton in the 1990s. In 1995 he did something which had Everton's stunned manager Joe Royle saying, *"punching his Italian marker on the jaw* isn't in his contract."

6 John Robertson was a winger who had the complete confidence of his manager, Brian Clough, at Nottingham Forest. Clough's bellowed instructions from the dug-out regularly included the command, "Give it to *The Golden Ball!"*

7 It isn't well known that in his early days at Manchester United, star No. 7 David Beckham spent a month on loan to Preston North End – where he discovered to his horror that he was expected to *run 100 metres in 11 seconds.*

8 Francisco Gento played for Real Madrid and Spain in the 1950s and 1960s. He's the only player so far to win six European Cup winner's medals. Gento already had a different collection of medals before a became a footballer, though – for Athletics. He was so fast he could *hardly walk*.

9 Oleg Blokhin spent 18 years (1969–1988) with Dynamo Kiev, winning eight USSR National Championships, two European Cup Winners' Cups (1975, 1986), a Super Cup (1975) and *the Fat Man* (the prize for the European Footballer of the Year) in 1975.

Answers:

1 Best *knocked the ball out of the referee's hands* after United had lost a League Cup semi-final to local rivals Manchester City.

2 Sanchez leapt up and settled the argument by *punching his Italian marker on the jaw*. What's more, the referee didn't even send him off for what had been a perfect left hook! Maybe he thought Italy's defender, Humberto Maschio, had only himself to blame; he should have known Sanchez's father had been Chilean and South American boxing champion.

I WANT A CLEAN FIGHT, NO BITING OR KICKING...

> ## THE SHOW YOUNGSTERS HOW TO PLAY THE GAME AWARD...
> **Leonel Sanchez.** When he retired, Sanchez concentrated on playing the game the right way. He set up football coaching schools for five to 12-year-olds.

3 It was something of a miracle that Garrincha could play at all because after a childhood illness he could *hardly walk*. But in spite of his badly twisted legs Garrincha ended playing 581 games for his club Botafogo and scoring 232 goals. He also played 60 times for Brazil – ending up on the losing side just once!

4 Littbarski's dream was that one day he'd beat all ten outfield players, dribble round the goalkeeper and *put the ball in the net with a back-heel.*

He never did manage it. What he did manage was to play for West Germany in the 1982, 1986 and 1990 World Cups, which was probably the next best thing.

5 *"Heading* isn't in his contract" was what Royle said after seeing Kanchelsis prove he Kan nod them into the net when he wants.

6 Clough's less than complimentary shout was, "Give it to *the Fat Man!*" It was an accurate assessment of Robertson's two main qualities. The fried-food lover may have been as round as a football but he could certainly dribble one as well. When Clough's team, Nottingham Forest, retained the European Cup in 1980 it was Jelly John who scored the winning goal.

7 Beckham discovered to his horror that he was expected to *wash his own football kit*. Life wasn't so glamorous as at United, where the players were used to leaving their smelly stuff in the changing room for somebody else to pick up.

8 Gento was so fast he could *run 100 metres in 11 seconds.* No wonder his nickname was "El Supersonico"!

9 Blokhin won *the Golden Ball.* He's the outstanding player in the history of Soviet football, scoring over 300 goals during his career with club and country.

Prize pen-pix: gorgeous George Best

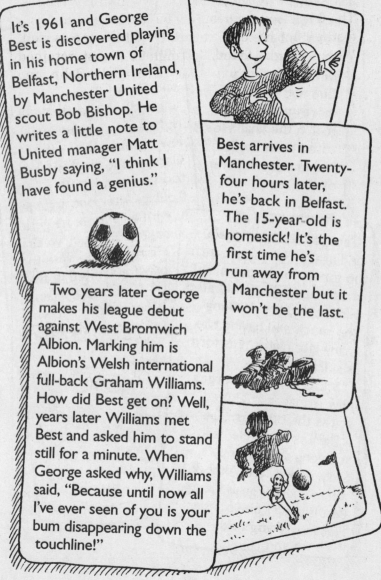

It's 1961 and George Best is discovered playing in his home town of Belfast, Northern Ireland, by Manchester United scout Bob Bishop. He writes a little note to United manager Matt Busby saying, "I think I have found a genius."

Best arrives in Manchester. Twenty-four hours later, he's back in Belfast. The 15-year-old is homesick! It's the first time he's run away from Manchester but it won't be the last.

Two years later George makes his league debut against West Bromwich Albion. Marking him is Albion's Welsh international full-back Graham Williams. How did Best get on? Well, years later Williams met Best and asked him to stand still for a minute. When George asked why, Williams said, "Because until now all I've ever seen of you is your bum disappearing down the touchline!"

The 17-year-old is also picked for his country, Northern Ireland.

In 1968 Best proves he's the best. Manchester United win the European Cup and George scores a decisive goal in the final. He's voted both English and European Player of the Year.

He's got fans in the most unlikely places. "I wish he had been born in England," said Sir Alf Ramsey, England's manager! Trouble is, he's also getting quite a few non-fans: the referees. George is losing his temper too often and getting into trouble. After one argument with a referee, he gets banned for four weeks. He returns in time to play for United in their FA Cup match against Northampton Town – and scores six goals in an 8-2 win!

George runs away again – and again. He doesn't turn up for a Northern Ireland match and misses a United game too. He's drinking too much and having too many late nights. His form is suffering.

Frank O'Farrell, George's new manager at United, states the obvious: "George is like a boy lost. He needs someone to help him."

Sadly, nobody can. After 361 games and 137 goals George Best is given a free transfer. He's just 27 years old.

He spends the next ten years or so playing for any team who hopes he might discover his old magic for them. The list includes Stockport County, Cork Celtic, Fulham, Hibernian, Bournemouth, some American teams like San Jose Earthquakes – and Ford Open Prison. He plays for them after being convicted for drunkenness.

In 1984 George Best plays his final first-class game. Since then virtually the whole football world has wondered how good he could have been. One of the few who didn't was his old manager, Matt Busby. He looked on the bright side, saying: "We had some problems with the wee fella, but I prefer to remember his genius. He had more ways of beating an opponent than any other player I have seen."

THE BIG BROTHERS PROBLEM

So you want to be a prize player? Well, are your mum and dad mad about football? No? Don't worry. It isn't always necessary to have football nuts as parents. Take Mr and Mrs Charles, whose sons John and Clive both played for West Ham United in the 1960s and 1970s. They were discovered by the club's talent scout, Wally St Pier. But when he turned up at their house and said he was a Chief Scout, Mrs Charles assumed he'd left his woggle and shorts at home and trotted off to tell her sons a Boy Scout leader had come to call!

DIB-DIB-DIB...

THE GIVE YOUR SONS A LESS CONFUSING NAME THAN YOU WERE LANDED WITH AWARD...
Mr Neville, father of Manchester United and England brothers Gary and Philip Neville. When his own parents were searching for a name they'd run out of ideas pretty quickly. Mr Neville's full name is Neville Neville!

A number of families have produced more than one prize player, though not always very successfully. The Clarke brothers, for instance, have been relegated so often they should have been miners instead of footballers...

- Allan Clarke (before a successful career with Leeds United) was relegated with Fulham in 1968. In June 1968 he moved to Leicester City – and went down again!
- Frank Clarke was with Carlisle when they dropped out of the old First Division in 1975.
- Derek Clarke was an Oxford United player when they fell into the old Third division in 1976.
- Kelvin Clarke was with Walsall when they followed the same path in 1979 (although he had an excuse – he only got into the team once!).
- Which left only youngest brother Wayne Clarke, who proved that anything the others could do, he could do just as well. Woeful Wayne went down from the old First Division twice, with Wolverhampton Wanderers in 1984 and Birmingham City in 1986.

First prize for a successful family almost certainly goes to the Milburn mob of Ashington, a small mining village in Northumberland. In the 1940s and 1950s fans could be confused by:

- Jackie Milburn, who played for Newcastle and England (1946–1957).
- George Milburn (Leeds and Chesterfield).
- Jack Milburn (Leeds and Bradford City).
- Jimmy Milburn (Leeds and Bradford Park Avenue).
- Stan Milburn (Chesterfield, Leicester and Rochdale).

and, perhaps the most important of the lot...

● Miss Cissie Milburn (who only played in the back garden).

So how come Cissie Milburn was really important? Because she went on to bear two sons who became international footballers themselves. Their names? To find that out you'll have to solve the clues in this big brothers quiz.

The table gives you the first names of six pairs of prize brothers who all played for their countries. Solve the clues to discover the brothers' last names and the country they represented.

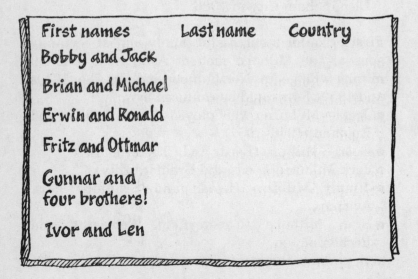

First names	Last name	Country
Bobby and Jack		
Brian and Michael		
Erwin and Ronald		
Fritz and Ottmar		
Gunnar and four brothers!		
Ivor and Len		

Clues:

1 When Cissie Milburn married she changed her last name to Charlton; she named one of her sons Robert.

2 Brian and his brother both played for Denmark; their surname isn't Nordahl.

3 Ottmar played for the winning team in the 1954 World Cup Final in which Hungary were beaten 3-2 by Germany.

4 The Allchurch brothers played for Wales, a country with the leek as its favourite vegetable – unlike Gunnar's brothers, who were all Swedes.

5 The English brothers weren't Erwin and Ronald or Ivor and Len.

6 Finn Laudrup, father of two sons, was also an international footballer – not for Finland, but for Denmark.

7 The Koeman brothers, neither of whom was called Len, won 1988 European Championship winner's medals with Holland.

8 A man named Walter lifted the trophy in the 1954 World Cup Final.

Answers: (number in brackets gives related clue).

First Names	Last Name	Country
Bobby and Jack	Charlton (1)	England (5)
Brian and Michael	Laudrup (6)	Denmark (2)
Erwin and Ronald	Koeman (7)	Holland (7)
Fritz and Ottmar	Walter (8)	Germany (3)
Gunnar and four brothers	Nordahl (8)	Sweden (4)
Ivor and Len	Allchurch (7 and 3)	Wales (7)

Bobby and Jack Charlton are probably England's most famous footballing brothers, having both been in the England team which won the World Cup in 1966. Bobby was a striker, Jack a defender – and Cissie Milburn was the mum who helped them get started. Not only did she play football with them, she even made their first kit. With money and materials being in short supply after World War II, she sat down and knitted her boys pairs of red and white socks – and made black shorts out of old curtains!

I DON'T THINK MUCH OF YOURS

Brian and Michael Laudrup both played for Denmark. Michael was the older brother and looked like he was going to be top man after he won a European Cup winner's medal with his club Barcelona in 1992. But after a big row with Denmark's manager he was left out of his country's team for that summer's European Championships.

Who took his place? Little bro Brian – and Denmark went on to win the tournament!

Ronald and Erwin Koeman were both in Holland's victorious European Championship-winning team of 1988. They too had a footballer for a dad. They even started their careers playing for his old team, Groningen.

Fritz and Ottmar Walter both played in Germany's forward line in the 1954 World Cup Final. No doubt who was big brother, though. Fritz was captain, so he took the penalties and even the corners! But Ottmar got his own back. He hit four goals during the tournament – one more than his brother.

THE NOT QUITE AS GOOD AS MICHAEL COLEMAN BUT STILL PRETTY GOOD AWARD...

Fritz Walter. After he'd retired, Fritz wrote a number of successful football books – which he probably made Ottmar read in bed!

Gunnar Nordahl won an Olympic Games medal for football when Sweden won the competition in 1948. After that he turned professional and went to Italy, where, with Milan and Roma, he was the Italian league's top scorer five times. What did his four brothers do? They stayed at home and played in the Swedish first division. Well, Mr and Mrs Nordahl had to go and watch somebody, didn't they?

Ivor and Len Allchurch were both forwards who had long playing careers during the 1950s and 1960s with neither of them winning a medal. Ivor hit 251 goals for Swansea, Newcastle and Cardiff and won 68 caps for Wales. Len scored fewer goals (108) and won fewer caps for Wales (11). Maybe that's because he was younger than Ivor – by four years.

THE EQUAL BROTHERS AWARD...

Victor and Vyacheslav Chanov were brothers who didn't have any reason to argue. They were both goalkeepers and in 1982 they both won places in the USSR squad for the World Cup. What's more, they both played an equal number of games – none! Neither of them could dislodge the first choice goalkeeper, Rinat Dassajev.

STUNNING STRIKERS

As footballers have said ever since the first sitter was missed, "At the end of the day it's goals what count, y'know. Get 'em and you're over the moon, but miss 'em and you're as sick as a parrot."

That's why the players who really win the prizes are the strikers. If they score, everybody wants to know them. Miss, and the only prize the fans want to give them is a booby prize.

Record goal grabbers: no-prize Payne and lithe Leonidas

Back in 1936, Joe Payne hadn't qualified for any sort of prize at all. The midfielder was stuck in the reserves at Luton Town – and, as they were stuck in the old Third Division, his chances of becoming famous seemed pretty slim. Then, on Easter Monday, Joe got the call. He was playing in the first team, against Bristol Rovers...

And that's exactly what Joe Payne did. In his first-ever game as centre-forward he banged the ball into the net once, twice, three times … and didn't stop until he'd scored ten! Luton won 12-0 and Joe Payne had found his position. The following season Payne hit a Luton record of 55 goals and the team were promoted.

Leonidas da Silva, known simply as Leonidas in his country, Brazil, was another striker who left his mark on history. He was top scorer in the 1938 World Cup with eight goals in four games, four of them coming in one game. But what the fans wanted to see almost more than goals was a leaping Leonidas showing off his stunning new trick. Here's how to try it for yourself – but not in the playground! You'll need something soft to land on:

STAND IN THE MIDDLE OF THE PENALTY AREA-FACING AWAY FROM THE GOAL!

GET SOMEBODY TO WHACK THE BALL ACROSS HIGH IN THE AIR.

WHACK!

AS IT COMES OVER, LEAP UPWARDS - BUT NOT TO HEAD IT. LAUNCH YOURSELF INTO A BACKWARDS SOMERSAULT SO YOUR FEET GO UP FIRST!

NOW PRETEND YOU'RE PEDALLING A BICYCLE- NOT FORWARDS BUT BACKWARDS AND...

WITH YOUR RIGHT FOOT, KICK THE BALL - NOT OUT OF THE SCHOOL BUT INTO THE GOAL!

Done it? Well done! You've just reproduced the trick Leonidas became famous for – the "bicycle kick".

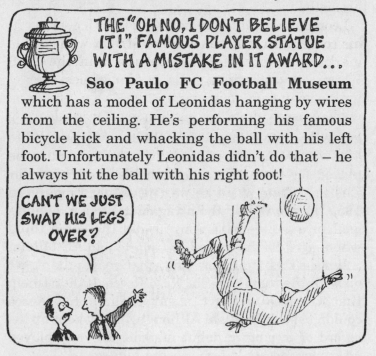

THE "OH NO, I DON'T BELIEVE IT!" FAMOUS PLAYER STATUE WITH A MISTAKE IN IT AWARD...

Sao Paulo FC Football Museum which has a model of Leonidas hanging by wires from the ceiling. He's performing his famous bicycle kick and whacking the ball with his left foot. Unfortunately Leonidas didn't do that – he always hit the ball with his right foot!

CAN'T WE JUST SWAP HIS LEGS OVER?

Net masters: cool Jim and silky da Silva

Jimmy Greaves made his debut for Chelsea aged 17 and inside two years had become the club's – and the First Division's – top scorer. In 1960–1961 he hit 43 goals, including six hat tricks and a five.

Greaves was a stealthy striker, nipping in to slot the ball home rather than blasting in rocket shots. What do you do if you get a good chance to score in a match – get excited, rush and miss? Greaves never did:

"He was no more excited in front of goal than he was cleaning his teeth in the morning."

– Jimmy Hill, TV presenter

Goal-grabber Greaves kept an amazing sequence going throughout his career. Whenever he moved to a new team he scored a goal in the first game he played for them. He scored in his first match for Chelsea. Then, when he was picked for England in 1959, he scored for them (against Peru, England's goal in a 4-1 defeat). And he did the same thing when, aged 23, he moved to Italy to join AC Milan.

It wasn't a happy time, though. Greaves didn't get on with the team's coach, Nero Rocco. It didn't help that Greaves couldn't speak Italian and Rocco couldn't speak English! Although Jimmy kept up his record of scoring in debut matches, he only played 14 games for AC Milan, scoring nine goals.

JIMMY AND NERO SEEM TO HAVE FOUND A COMMON LANGUAGE!

Just a year later Greaves was back in England, signing for Tottenham Hotspur. He showed his delight in the only way he knew how. His first game for Tottenham was against Blackpool – and he scored a hat trick! They were the first three of the 220 goals he scored in 322 games for Tottenham. In the nine years he was with them, Jimmy was top scorer every time!

For England he blasted 44 goals in 57 games – but his international career ended in heartbreak. After being injured in a group game during the 1966 World Cup finals, Jimmy lost his place in the side to a certain Geoff Hurst. All he could do was watch as Hurst hit his famous hat trick in England's 4-2 win against West Germany in the final. Gloomy Greaves was the only member of the 22-man squad who didn't turn up for the posh hotel celebration that night. He never played for England again.

In 1970, in the twilight of his career, Jimmy moved to West Ham. He played only 38 games and, for him, scored just a puny 13 goals. Surprise, surprise – two of them came in his first game for his new club!

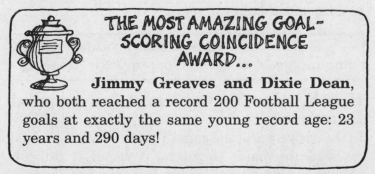

THE MOST AMAZING GOAL-SCORING COINCIDENCE AWARD...

Jimmy Greaves and Dixie Dean, who both reached a record 200 Football League goals at exactly the same young record age: 23 years and 290 days!

During his career with Benfica in the 1960s there was very little doubt about who was going to be the Portuguese league's top scorer. Eusebio da Silva Ferreira (known just by his first name from the time he burst on the scene in 1961) took that place every season from 1964 to 1968! In 1968 he became the first-ever winner of the Golden Boot Award as Europe's top goalscorer, and was also voted European Player of the Year. As if that wasn't enough, electric Eusebio was top scorer in the 1966 World Cup in England.

And yet one of the best-known memories of Eusebio is to do with a goal he *didn't* score. With just a few minutes to go in the 1968 European Cup Final between Manchester United and Benfica, and the score at 1-1, Eusebio sprinted through the defence and had only United's goalkeeper Alex Stepney to beat. Racing into the penalty area he blasted the ball goalwards – only to see Stepney guess which way it was going and pluck it out of the air. What did Eusebio do?

a) Pat Stepney on the back.

b) Pretend his boot had come loose.

c) Drop to his knees in tears.

Answer: a) Eusebio wasn't only a stunning striker, he was a super sport.

Hot header Tommy and hot-headed Romario

In the early days of the game, players weren't allowed to head the ball. They'd have found it difficult anyway, because they used to wear hats and caps.

Nowadays, football is the only ball sport in which players deliberately use their heads to try and score (unlike cricket, in which you can score runs if the ball hits you on the head, but nobody in their right mind does it deliberately!). That's why star strikers are often hot headers of the ball. But does it explain why some of them are very hot-headed as well?

Tommy Lawton burst onto the scene as a 17-year-old with Burnley, scoring a hat trick in his first league game – though nobody should have been surprised. You think you're a good striker? In his first three years of schoolboy football with Folds Road Central School in Bolton, Tommy Lawton scored 570 goals!

He soon joined Everton, becoming the club's youngest goalscorer – a record that lasted for 70 years until Wayne Rooney broke it in October 2002. He also managed almost a goal a game for England, hitting 22 goals in just 23 games. One of those goals, against Portugal in 1947, hit the back of the net in a record 17 seconds!

111

Lawton's great talent was heading. He made goals for others and nodded in plenty himself. Here's how to do it terrific Tommy's way in your next school match...

WHEN YOUR TEAM WINS A CORNER, DRIFT INTO THE PENALTY AREA.
AS THE BALL COMES OVER, JUMP GRACEFULLY UPWARDS...

RISING HIGHER THAN EVERY DEFENDER. AT THE TOP OF YOUR LEAP...

...MAKE IT APPEAR AS THOUGH YOU'RE HOVERING AND...SHOUT AT THE OTHER TEAM'S GOALKEEPER...
TOP CORNER!
ER?

THEN, AS THE BALL ARRIVES HEAD IT EXACTLY WHERE YOU SAID, IN THE TOP CORNER!

That's what Tommy Lawton once did to Charlton's goalkeeper Sam Bartram!

Yes, he was a hot header all right. Unfortunately, he was also hot-headed. When England's first-ever manager, Walter Winterbottom, met the players and suggested they have a meeting to talk tactics, Lawton replied: "You're going to tell me how to score goals? You've got another think coming. Goodnight!"

He didn't play many more games for England after that! He was a star, though, and fetched huge transfer fees whenever he went to a new club. In 1947, when he moved from First Division Chelsea to Third Division Notts County the fee was a record £20,000 – "only" worth £475,000 now, but a massive amount in those days. Did the club get their money's worth? You bet. When Lawton left five years later, the team had been promoted and their average crowd had risen from 9,000 to 35,000! Somebody had his hot head screwed on right!

Romario da Souza Faria – known simply as Romario – hit five goals for Brazil when they won the World Cup in 1994. There wasn't a hot header amongst them. Nicknamed "O Baixinho" (the Little Man), Romario's skill was with his feet. In matches he was as cool-headed as they come – but off the field it was totally different. Romario was always in trouble because he had his own hot-headed ideas about training. What were they?
a) He liked to party before training.
b) He liked to party after training.
c) He liked to party instead of training.

> **Answer: b)** always, **a)** quite often and **c)** whenever he got the chance!

Romario started his partying career at a young age. He was thrown out of Brazil's *Youth* World Cup squad for staying out too late! Even so, his goalscoring feats led most managers to look the other way. One who didn't was the gloriously named

Wanderley Luxemburgo. He was in charge of the team Romario joined straight after his 1994 World Cup triumph, Brazilian league side Flamengo. When Romario strolled in he was disgusted to discover that Luxemburgo expected him to train normally, like every other player at the club. What happened next?

a) Romario refused – and was sacked.

b) Romario refused – and Luxemburgo was sacked.

THE PLAYER WITH THE HOTTEST NAME AWARD...

Nolberto Solano, the Peruvian international who joined Newcastle United in 1998 and has since irritated plenty of Premiership defences by racing through from midfield to score against them. In Spanish, the "Solano" is a scorching wind carrying fine dust which irritates people and makes them feel giddy!

Scoring away: cheerful Charles and Kev of the kop

Nowadays it's common for a prize player to leave home and join a club in a foreign country. It wasn't always like this. In the early days of the game in Britain, "playing abroad" meant a Scottish footballer joining an English club! Jimmy Greaves didn't enjoy playing in another country, but here are two strikers who showed they could score at home or away...

John Charles was a rarity, a prize player who could play just as well in defence or attack. He spent the first eight years of his career with Leeds United, scoring 150 goals in 257 games. One season he hit a record 42 goals – in between playing for his country, Wales, as a star central defender!

His move abroad was to the Italian club, Juventus. You'd have thought that the Leeds bosses would have been sad to see him go. Apparently not. The signing took place in a hotel room. Charles had gone there with two Leeds United directors to meet Juventus boss Umberto Agnelli. After some haggling the deal was done. Agnelli wrote out a cheque for the transfer fee (£65,000 – about twice the British transfer record at the time) and put it on a table while he had a chat to Charles. When the two men turned round, the Leeds directors had gone without even saying goodbye, taking the cheque with them!

WE'VE GOT THE CASH!

John Charles was quickly given a nickname by the Juventus fans. They called him "Il Buon Gigante" – the Gentle Giant. This wasn't because he was a gentle player, but because he was a fair one. He was never sent off or booked. With Juventus he won three Italian championships

and two Italian cups, scoring 93 goals in 155 games. Pretty good in a country where they thought 1-0 was a high score!

He gave some advice to any other players who might fancy following him:

"Tell yourself you're getting well paid and put up with the strictness and soul-destroying defensive football. Then you will have a fine time."

Kevin Keegan was also an overseas success. After six great seasons with Liverpool during which he'd won two League Championships, the FA Cup, two UEFA Cups and the European Cup, Keegan made his move to Hamburg in Germany in 1977. He did well, helping Hamburg win the Bundesliga title and reach the European Cup Final in 1980. His German adventure didn't start well, though. As part of the transfer deal, Hamburg played a friendly match against Liverpool – and were hammered 6-0! The happy Liverpool fans sang at Kevin, "You should have stayed at Anfield."

Things improved, though. Hamburg's fans thought a lot of Keegan, partly because he learned to speak German. Who taught him most at first?

a) His team-mates.

b) Local children.

c) His neighbours.

Answer: b) He would try out his German on them while he signed autographs. The early words he learned from his team-mates were mostly swear words!

Kevin always was a popular player. During his time in Hamburg the local newspaper ran a comic strip, starring "Super Kevin"!

In 1980 Keegan came back to England for successful spells with both Southampton and Newcastle – helping Newcastle win promotion back to the old First Division. But the German people didn't forget him. When Keegan hung up his boots and became a manager instead, Hamburg fans hoped he might come back to them. (He didn't, though – he went back to Newcastle.) As Christian Reichert, chairman of the Hamburg Supporters' Federation, said: "I knew 500 people who would have walked barefoot to London to plead for Keegan's return."

That's called being popular!

THE MOST ONE-SIDED AWARD-WINNERS AWARD...

Kevin Keegan. When a TV programme called "Who Is The Greatest?" pitted Kevin Keegan against gorgeous George Best the 12-person jury voted 11 to one for classy Kevin. It was only later that the TV company discovered the person they'd asked to pick the jury had been the organizer of a Kevin Keegan Fan Club!

Stunningly stupid striking celebrations

Nowadays, it seems, simply scoring a spectacular goal isn't enough. To really stand out from the crowd, a stunning striker has got to have a spectacularly stupid way of celebrating his goal as well.

The strickers and their celebrations have got mixed up. Use the clues to match them correctly.

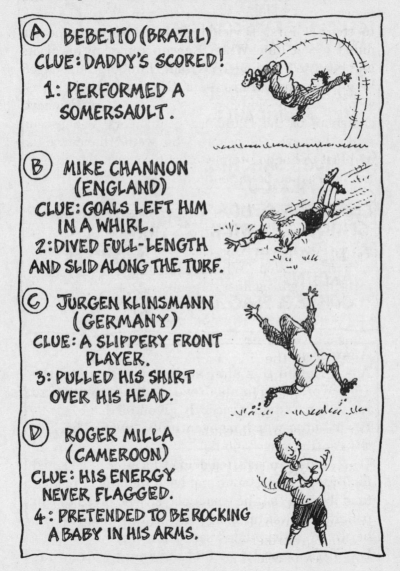

Ⓐ BEBETTO (BRAZIL)
CLUE: DADDY'S SCORED!
1: PERFORMED A SOMERSAULT.

Ⓑ MIKE CHANNON (ENGLAND)
CLUE: GOALS LEFT HIM IN A WHIRL.
2: DIVED FULL-LENGTH AND SLID ALONG THE TURF.

Ⓒ JURGEN KLINSMANN (GERMANY)
CLUE: A SLIPPERY FRONT PLAYER.
3: PULLED HIS SHIRT OVER HIS HEAD.

Ⓓ ROGER MILLA (CAMEROON)
CLUE: HIS ENERGY NEVER FLAGGED.
4: PRETENDED TO BE ROCKING A BABY IN HIS ARMS.

E FABRIZIO RAVANELLI
(ITALY)

CLUE: THE FANS COULD SEE IT, EVEN IF HE COULDN'T.

5: SWUNG HIS RIGHT ARM ROUND AND ROUND LIKE A WINDMILL.

F HUGO SANCHEZ
(MEXICO)

CLUE: GOALS PUT A SPRING IN HIS STEP.

6: DID A DANCE AROUND A CORNER FLAG.

Answers:

A – 4 He did this after scoring for Brazil in the 1994 World Cup finals. It was a gooey message to his wife who'd only recently given birth.

B – 5 – after which he eventually "swung" back to the centre "circle", ho-ho!

C – 2 Klinsmann started doing this after he'd signed for Tottenham Hotspur and been told that England fans thought that he was a player who dived to win penalties. It was his little joke – but the many teams he scored against didn't see it that way!

D – 6 It's a wonder he had the energy; Milla was

the oldest player to score in the World Cup finals in 1994, when he was 42.

E – 3 Good job he didn't do it before he scored!

F – 1 Sanchez got a lot of practice. In the late 1980s and early 1990s he was the top Spanish league goalscorer five seasons in row. Mind you, he'd had a good somersault teacher – his sister! She represented Mexico at gymnastics in the 1976 Olympic Games.

THE PLAYING OUT OF HIS SKIN AWARD...

Diego Forlan of Manchester United and Uruguay who, after scoring for United against West Ham in 2002, whipped off his shirt – only to find that it was so tangled up he couldn't get back on again. After joining in the re-started game, Forlan eventually had to give up and leave the pitch for the United trainer to sort him out.

DO YOU WANT ME TO DO UP YOUR LACEY-WACEYS AS WELL?

Prize pen-pix: William Ralph "Dixie" Dean

Dixie Dean was the Michael Owen of his era, except that he scored more goals – and played for Everton rather than Liverpool.

In the 1927–1928 season, aged 21, he scored 60 league goals in 39 matches. That is still a record.

Forty of those goals were scored with his head – which was amazing because in 1926 he'd had a metal plate put in his skull after fracturing it in a motorbike accident. Dixie was a hard nut, all right!

Dixie scored 12 goals in his first five games for England (2,3,2,2,3).

His total record was 18 goals in 16 Internationals.

One of Dean's great rivals was Elisha Scott, the Liverpool goalkeeper. The day before the two teams were due to meet, Dean would send Scott a note warning him to be ready for a pasting next day. He hoped the thought would keep Elisha awake all night so that he wouldn't be so sharp during the game!

Dixie Dean's heading ability led to a favourite (invented) story about how, when Dean and Elisha Scott met in the street one day, Dean nodded "hello" – and Scott automatically dived into the gutter to save an imaginary ball!

Arsenal wanted to buy Dean from Everton and told the club they'd pay anything they asked. Everton refused to sell. Dean stayed an Everton fan to his dying day. Literally: he died at Everton's ground after watching his old team play against Liverpool in 1980.

FIRST-PRIZE PLAYERS

Try this experiment at school – not just with your friends, but with your teachers and dinner-ladies as well. Ask them if they've heard of any of these four people:

a) David Beckham.

b) Diego Maradona.

c) Michael Owen.

d) Edson Arantes do Nascimento (if they go blurry-eyed on this one, just use his nickname, "Pelé", instead).

The chances are that, unless they've been living in an underground bunker for the past 50 years, they'll say "yes" to all four of them – even if they hate football and think "offside" is a kind of haircut.

Why? Because these four footballers have become what every footballer (and football fan) dreams of becoming: a legend.

Question: In 2000, the international football organization, FIFA, decided to celebrate the millennium by holding two votes for the greatest footballer of all time. The first vote was amongst the players and officials of every country. The second was a vote held on the Internet. Which of the four players won?

> **Answer:** The official FIFA vote was won by Pelé (with 75% of the votes). The Internet vote was won by Maradona (with 54%).

Will Beckham and Owen win if they hold another contest in the year 3000? How would you have voted in 2000 if you'd had the chance? Weigh up the top foul football facts about each of the legendary four as we go head-to-head with the heroes!

Peerless Pelé v Brilliant Beckham

Even legends were young once...

Pelé grew up in Baura, a poor area of Brazil. He didn't have a pair of football boots or a ball. Instead he played barefoot with a bundle of rags tied up with string. When he finally did get a real football all his neighbours quickly knew it. One of his first tricks was to bust the only lamp in the street!

David Beckham lived in Essex, and would spend hours practising in the local park. He was spotted by Manchester United when he won a football skills competition as a 12-year-old and had the prize

awarded to him on the pitch at Old Trafford. United were always the club he wanted to play for. He used to turn up for schoolboy training sessions at Tottenham Hotspur wearing his Manchester United replica kit!

Reaching the big-time

If you're going to be a legend, you'll have to get yourself spotted before you can shave. Pelé played his first league game for top Brazilian team Santos when he was 15 years old.

In comparison, David Beckham had to wait ages until he made his first-team debut with Manchester United. He was 17 years old when he came on as a substitute in a match against Brighton. It wasn't a big game though – a second round, second leg match in the Rumbelows Cup! He had to wait another two years before making his Premiership home debut against Leeds United.

Club compilation

Apart from the final few years he spent playing in the North American league, Pelé stayed with Santos for his whole career. He won championships in Brazil and in both 1962 and 1963 Santos became World Club Champions.

David Beckham's sideboard must already be groaning with the medals he's won. Starting as a FA Youth Cup winner in 1992, he's since collected medals for being FA Premiership champion, FA Cup winner and European Champions' League winner.

Playing for their countries

Here's a mind-boggling thing to do. Subtract your age from 17. Got the answer? Well, that's how long you've got left if you're to copy Pelé. He was just 17 years old when he scored twice in the 1958 World Cup Final! He made his international debut when he was 16. In the 1962 competition, he was injured after one game, but picked up a winner's medal. In 1966 he was fouled so badly that he had to be carried off (it's not always fun being a legend) and Brazil came nowhere. But in 1970 Pelé was back in the side, scoring a great goal as Brazil won again. Three World Cup winner's medals – legendary!

You've got another four years to play with if you only want to copy David Beckham. He didn't make his England debut until he was 20. At 25 he was made captain. Pelé never became captain of Brazil – but then David Beckham hasn't yet won the World Cup. In 1998 his team went out in the second round against Argentina (and he got sent off!) and in 2002 they lost in the quarter-final (to Brazil, grrr!).

Most famous goal

Pelé himself says that the goal he remembers most is a penalty he scored for Santos in a floodlit league match. As he put the ball on the spot he suddenly felt more nervous than he'd ever felt before about taking a penalty kick. As he ran in, the goal suddenly seemed smaller. Pelé side-footed it to his right, and the goalkeeper (who might well have been in trouble if he'd saved the kick) dived the other way. So, what was all the fuss about? It was Pelé's 1,000th goal in top-class football, that's what!

In a group match in the 1970 World Cup, Pelé had just missed scoring with an outrageous shot from the half-way line. On the opening day of the 1996–1997 season, in a league match against Wimbledon, David Beckham tried the same trick – the difference being that in his case the ball sailed over the despairing goalkeeper's head and into the net!

When you're a legend people sometimes say really nice things about you...

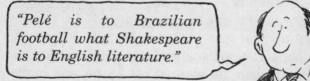

"Pelé is to Brazilian football what Shakespeare is to English literature."

– Joao Saldanha, ex-Brazil manager.

"Beckham is brilliant. He is very good technically. He has great awareness, a great shot and of course he provides those fantastic crosses."

– Marcello Lippi, Juventus coach.

...and sometimes they can say really dumb things about you

"If Pelé hadn't been born a man he'd have been born a ball."

– Armando Nogueira, excitable and confused journalist.

"Beckham has two feet, which a lot of players don't have nowadays."

– short-sighted TV pundit, Jimmy Hill.

Sometimes legends can say pretty dumb things themselves...

"I think that France, Germany, Spain and Holland will join England in the semi-finals."

– Pelé, forgetting that even in his day semi-finals only had enough room for four teams.

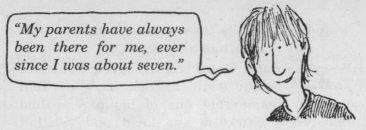

"My parents have always been there for me, ever since I was about seven."

– David Beckham, forgetting the first six years of his life.

...but they can also say things that show they're more than footballers

"Every kid around the world who plays soccer wants to be Pelé. I have a great responsibility to show them not just how to be like a soccer player but how to be like a man."

– Pelé.

"It's scary to read things like that, you know, being the best player in England, but it gives me confidence. I'm not going to go around shouting about things that people say about me, but it's nice that they say it."

– David Beckham.

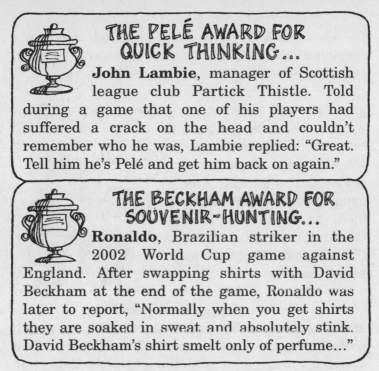

THE PELÉ AWARD FOR QUICK THINKING...

John Lambie, manager of Scottish league club Partick Thistle. Told during a game that one of his players had suffered a crack on the head and couldn't remember who he was, Lambie replied: "Great. Tell him he's Pelé and get him back on again."

THE BECKHAM AWARD FOR SOUVENIR-HUNTING...

Ronaldo, Brazilian striker in the 2002 World Cup game against England. After swapping shirts with David Beckham at the end of the game, Ronaldo was later to report, "Normally when you get shirts they are soaked in sweat and absolutely stink. David Beckham's shirt smelt only of perfume..."

Magical Maradona v Mercurial Michael

Even legends were young once...

Another way of becoming a legend is to get your own TV programme when you're nine years old! That's what Diego Armando Maradona did. Born in Buenos Aires in Argentina, he became a TV regular, showing off his ball-juggling skills. By the time he was 11, diddy Diego had formed his own football team with a group of friends. Their name? The Little

Onions – maybe because they made their opponents cry so much. The team were so successful that top club Argentinos Juniors signed the whole team.

Legends can't afford to hang about. Michael Owen was also doing big things by the time he was 11. He'd been playing in an under-11 schools team since he was seven but when he finally caught up with the rest of them he broke the scoring record for Deeside Primary Schools with 79 goals in a single season.

Reaching the big-time

Maradona played his first Argentine league match with Argentinos Juniors aged 15; by the time he'd scored his first league goal, though, his birthday had been and gone, and he was an oldie of 16.

Michael Owen joined the Liverpool FC School of Excellence aged 11 and hasn't left the club since. He was a regular in their youth team from age 15, winning the Youth FA Cup with them. He broke into the league side in 1997, aged 17 – and hit 30 goals in his first season.

Club compilation

Maradona was a good mover, and not only on the pitch. During his career he played in Argentina, winning the championship with Boca Juniors; in Spain, winning both the Spanish Cup and the

European Cup Winners' Cup with Barcelona; and in Italy, winning two Italian championships and the UEFA Cup with Napoli.

Owen hasn't gone anywhere – yet. What's more, until 2000–2001 he hadn't won anything with Liverpool's first team either. Then, in a single season, the club lifted the Worthington Cup, the FA Cup, the UEFA Cup and the European Super Cup!

Playing for their countries

In February 1977, at the age of 17, Diego played his first match for Argentina but his chance to do a Pelé vanished when he was left out of the Argentine squad for the 1978 World Cup – and his country went on to win it. He had to settle for captaining the Argentine Youth team to victory in their own World Cup in 1979. He was back for the real thing in 1986, though, lifting the trophy as Argentina won the World Cup again. But it all ended in tears. Maradona failed a drugs test (not for the first time) at the 1994 World Cup finals. At the age of 34 his international career was over. Magical, maddening Maradona had played 90 times and scored 33 goals.

Michael Owen's international record started with a bang when, aged 18 years and two months, he became the youngest player in the 20th century to play for England. Since then he's been in the World Cup sides of 1998 and 2002, winning (like David Beckham) nothing – yet.

Most famous goal

Deadly Diego qualifies as having two famous goals, not one. What's more, they both came in the same match – against England in the 1986 World Cup finals. For the first he leapt high into the air ... and punched the ball into the net! For the second, he picked the ball up in his own half and dribbled through the entire England defence to score. This goal was recently voted the "World Cup Goal of the Century" in a recent poll hosted on FIFA's official website. The first goal? That's regularly been voted the Cheat of the Century by England fans!

So whose goal came second in the "World Cup Goal of the Century" vote? The one scored by Michael Owen in 1998 – against, amazingly, Argentina! On that occasion it was Owen who picked the ball up on the halfway line, outpacing one defender and beating another before scoring with a rocket shot.

"*It's been replayed hundreds of times on TV and I've been asked to talk about it hundreds of times more, but I never get tired of seeing it or describing it.*"

– Michael Owen, showing that he thought it was a pretty good goal as well.

When you're a legend people sometimes say really nice things about you (unless they can't forget you once scored a cheat's goal)...

"*Pelé had nearly everything. Maradona has everything. He works harder, does more and is more skilful. Trouble is that he'll be remembered for another reason. He bends the rules to suit himself.*"

– Ex-England manager, Sir Alf Ramsey in 1986.

"*My favourite player is Michael Owen.*"

– Pelé in 2002.

...And sometimes they can say really dumb things about you (especially when you're only 5ft 8ins/1.73m tall)

> *"I don't think there's anyone bigger or smaller than Maradona."*

– Kevin Keegan, being clever and dumb in the same breath.

> *"Michael Owen isn't the tallest of lads, but his height more than makes up for that."*

– TV pundit and ex-Liverpool player Mark Lawrenson just managing the dumb part.

Sometimes legends can say pretty dumb things themselves

> *"It was a little bit the head of Maradona, a little bit the Hand of God."*

– perhaps the most famous World Cup quote, and probably still the dumbest.

> *"I was alone up front, with Danny Murphy playing between me, myself and the midfield."*

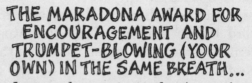

– Michael Owen, seeing double.

THE MARADONA AWARD FOR ENCOURAGEMENT AND TRUMPET-BLOWING (YOUR OWN) IN THE SAME BREATH...

Diego Maradona, who wrote to the Argentine newspaper *Ole* before England met his country in the 2002 World Cup: "Argentina needs you and I have huge faith in you. I know you are going to hoist our blue and white flag as I once did. I want you to know I will never abandon you."

THE OWEN AWARD FOR NATURE STUDIES (NOT)...

Craig Brown, ex-Scotland manager. Referring to Owen's speed off the mark Brown said, "He's got the legs of a salmon!"

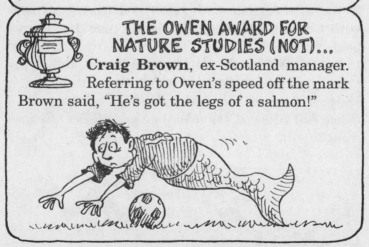

THE PRIZE PORTRAYAL QUIZ

Newspaper reports, TV interviews, fans' nicknames – when you're a footballer you can't avoid finding out what people think about you. Do they think you're a prize player ... or do they think you're a prize twerp?

In this collection of quotes and nicknames the word PRIZE *isn't* the word that was really used. Replace it with the correct one from this list of prize words:

> *assassin, big, bum, cosmonaut, eel, golden,*
> *mortar, night, paper, wonder*

1 Sandor Kocsis of Hungary was top scorer in the 1954 World Cup. He was so good in the air they called him *The Man With The PRIZE Head.*

2 Kenny Dalglish had great goalscoring careers with Celtic and Liverpool, hitting over 100 league goals with each. He wasn't big, but he was very hard to knock off the ball. Nottingham Forest and Derby County manager Brian Clough thought he knew Dalglish's secret: *"He had a PRIZE that came down below his knees; that's where he got all his strength from."*

138

3 Nobby Stiles was only a little defender for Manchester United and England in the 1960s but his tackling was so murderous one opposition manager called him *The PRIZE*.

4 Omar Sivori, a clever forward who played for Juventus in the 1950s, liked showing off and making defenders look silly. That's why fans called him *PRIZE Head*.

5 Sometimes football writing in one language gives a different picture when translated into another language. In saying what a star Oleg Blokhin was in winning 100 caps for the Soviet Union, the German magazine *Kicker* described him as *The PRIZE of the Football Horizon.*

6 Matthias Sindelar was a star striker for the Austrian team of the 1930s, but because he looked too skinny to be a footballer he was known as *The Man of PRIZE*.

7 Bill "Tiny" Foulke, the 140 kg keeper, was called a lot of things because of his size. One of the kindest described him as *"a PRIZE to everyone who visits the classic grounds of the game"*.

8 Bernabe Ferreyra was one of the earliest shooting stars in Argentina, banging in loads of goals for River Plate in the 1930s. Because of his cannonball shots he was nicknamed *The PRIZE*.

9 Steve Bloomer was one of England's earliest goalscorers. After hitting five goals in a match against Wales in 1896 he was described by one newspaper reporter as *"slippery as an PRIZE."*

10 Zbigniew Boniek won three European trophies with Juventus in the 1980s. The club President came up with a nickname for him after noticing he seemed to play his best in evening matches. It was *PRIZE Beauty*.

Answers:

1 Sandor Kocsis – *The Man With The Golden Head*. In 68 internationals for Hungary he scored 75 goals, including a record seven hat tricks.

2 Kenny Dalglish – *had a bum that came down below his knees* according to Clough (except that Clough didn't actually use the word "bum"). Wherever Dalglish actually did get his power, it worked for Scotland too. He ended his international career as equal top scorer with Denis Law.

3 Nobby Stiles – *The Assassin*. That was the word used by Otto Gloria, the manager of Benfica. Maybe 'orrible Otto was still annoyed because United had beaten his team in the European Cup Final. Then again, maybe he was confused after hearing what Nobby's dad did for a "living" – he was an undertaker!

COME ON, SON!

4 Omar Sivori – *Big Head*. He had good reason. Juventus paid a then world-record fee for him in 1957 and he was voted European Footballer of the Year in 1961.

5 Oleg Blokhin – *The Cosmonaut of the Football Horizon*! The magazine was obviously trying to say that Blokhin was a bloke whose play was out of this world!

6 Matthias Sindelar – *The Man of Paper*. His 27 in 43 games for Austria made his critics "wrap up" though!

7 Bill Foulke – *"A wonder to everyone who visits the classic grounds of the game."* (They were probably wondering how he got to be that big.)

8 Bernabe Ferreyra – *The Mortar*. He scored so many goals for his club, River Plate, that an Argentine newspaper once offered a gold medal to any goalkeeper who could stop him scoring!

9 Steve Bloomer – *"as slippery as an eel"*. (There's no evidence that he was any good at sliding tackles, though.)

10 Zbigniew Boniek – *"Night Beauty"*. He was picked for Poland and won a third-place medal in the 1982 World Cup, scoring a hat trick against Belgium in one of the group games. Defenders couldn't sleep when "Night Beauty" was around!

So there you are. In this book you've met over 125 different players. They've played in different positions, been of different shapes and different sizes. Maybe one of them has been your shape or your size or played in your position?

If that's the case, why not use him as your model? Keep practising – and who knows, the next time this book comes out it could feature an extra-special prize player. You!